QUEST FOR ETERNAL SUNSHINE

QUEST FOR ETERNAL SUNSHINE

A HOLOCAUST SURVIVOR'S JOURNEY
FROM DARKNESS TO LIGHT

MENDEK RUBIN & MYRA GOODMAN

SHE WRITES PRESS

Published 2020
Printed in the United States of America
ISBN: 978-1-63152-878-1
ISBN: 978-1-63152-879-8
Library of Congress Control Number: 2019914835

For information, address:
She Writes Press
1569 Solano Ave #546
Berkeley, CA 94707

Photographs on page 110 and 111 (top image) © Charles Rotmil
Interior design by Tabitha Lahr

She Writes Press is a division of SparkPoint Studio, LLC.

Mendek's Dedication:

To music, dance, laughter, and harmony.
And to the spark of life that animates us all.

Myra's Dedication:

For my parents, Mendek and Edith Rubin,
with boundless love and gratitude.

And for my children, Marea and Jeff Goodman,
and my niece, Nina Harmer—
may your grandpa's story and wisdom
always be a source of strength and inspiration.

CONTENTS

MYRA'S INTRODUCTION

When my father was on his deathbed, I sat by his side with my mother and daughter. We listened to beautiful classical music on an old cassette player, tapes my dad had made throughout his life of the melodies he loved best.

Even though my father was lying in a hospital bed, surrounded by bottles of medication in a room with a stained linoleum floor, I felt the magnificence of heaven. The air was different—charged with peace, light, and love. I sensed we were not alone.

Surprisingly, in the days leading up to his death, I'd developed a new relationship with my father. Although he could no longer speak and his body was beginning to shut down, it seemed as if his spirit was active and could actually communicate with me.

When I thought his death was still weeks away, I left for the weekend. While I was gone, I felt him urging me to return. I didn't know if it was really my dad or just an overactive imagination, but I had my answer when I went home early to find him in extreme pain and my eighty-four-year-old mother in a terrible state. His care was being mismanaged, and I was able to quickly remedy the situation.

A couple of evenings later, I drove the few miles to my house to take a short break. I was relaxing in my hot tub under the darkening sky when suddenly my father's spirit visited me, guided by a spirit that I somehow knew was his mother. They swooped down to share final blessings for our family. My father didn't speak in words, but I heard his messages clearly with senses I hadn't known I possessed—not the eyes and ears I had lived with for almost half a century. When I went back to my dad's bedside, the universe felt new to me. Boundaries I'd always believed in had dissolved, and I felt surprisingly fortified. My dad died peacefully a few hours later.

My daughter is a midwife, and this was her first death. She told me the magic in the room felt the same as when a baby is born.

The joy of my father's release was tangible. I believed he was reuniting with members of his family who had died long ago—people whose names and stories I did not know. Not yet.

—◊—

My father, Mendek Rubin, immigrated to America in 1946 after surviving three horrendous years in Nazi slave labor concentration camps—years during which his parents and four of his siblings were murdered in Auschwitz. At twenty-one, he arrived at Ellis Island with only a sixth-grade education. He didn't speak English or have any money or marketable skills. What he did have was a brilliant and creative mind.

Over the next forty years, Mendek's inventions revolutionized both the jewelry and packaged salad industries. But even more remarkable was how he applied his genius to his own psyche, figuring out innovative methods to heal the deep, unresolved emotional pain he carried from his early life.

By age sixty, my father had not only overcome the severe depression that had plagued him for decades, he'd also become the most peaceful and joyful person I've ever met. Just as he'd invented revolutionary ways to manufacture bracelet clasps and package salad greens, he had discovered how to be truly happy and free.

—m—

When I was a girl, everyone who knew my father called him "good-natured." No one in our family remembers him saying even one harsh word to any of us. He was always kind and patient, but he also knew how to have fun. Only the people closest to him—my mother, Edith, and his sole surviving sibling, Bronia— understood the depth of the despair he hid so well.

There was only one time that I sensed a bottomless darkness deep within him. After wandering into the kitchen late at night, I saw him standing by the sink, his head hanging down. I felt confused and anxious. Was there something wrong with my dad? My father was my sunshine. I couldn't bear to see him as anything but happy and strong, so I tried to put the image out of my mind.

Throughout my life, my dad was someone I could always rely on. When I was young, he tucked me in at night and listened to my childhood fears. As an adult, he worked hard to help make my business a success.

In the early days of Earthbound Farm, when most people thought my husband, Drew, and I were crazy to try to sell pre-washed organic salad in bags because it had never been done before, my dad never once questioned the viability of our concept. Not only did he invent ingenious equipment to wash and pack our delicate baby greens, he also provided a crash course in manufacturing—teaching us to think about assembly lines, scaling up, and the most efficient ways to achieve top quality. His quiet assurance gave us the confidence and faith to pursue our dreams.

Over the next dozen years, as our company grew from a tiny roadside produce stand into the largest grower of organic produce in the world, I became a very busy working mom with two young children. My parents helped me by babysitting almost every day.

After my father died in the fall of 2012, I missed him even more than I expected. I craved his smile, and the feel of his hand in mine. I regretted how much I didn't know about him and had never even thought to ask. I'd lost the opportunity to learn his history and delve into the philosophical theories and spiritual revelations he loved to share.

But at the same time, I continued to feel his presence. *Daddy, are you here with me? Is the light I feel coming from you?*

Then one day, while sorting through his belongings, I found the unfinished manuscript of a book he'd worked on for many years, a work he'd titled *In Quest of the Eternal Sunshine*. It was the same manuscript he'd asked me to edit decades ago, during a hectic era when I was caring for two young children and a fast-growing business. I'd worked on the manuscript for a few days, but it had required more time than I could possibly devote, so I'd set it aside—temporarily, I thought at the time. In the intervening years, however, I'd completely forgotten it existed.

Now, I was riveted. I had a deep yearning to understand my father and uncover his secrets.

Night after night, I sat at my dining room table, tears streaming down my face as I soaked in my father's words. I learned so many things about him that I'd never known before. His writings were honest and intimate. While my father had always appeared calm and mild-mannered in person, on the page he expressed himself boldly and passionately.

What shocked me the most was the intensity of the pain that had suffocated my dad for much of his life: feeling unworthy, in despair, afraid of both living and dying. Following the Holocaust, the universe felt hostile to him, human existence pointless.

For forty-five years, Mendek was mired in feelings of hopelessness and fear—until, one day, he made a declaration of war against a life he found wanting. Refusing to waste his remaining years estranged from himself and the world at large, my father embarked upon an extraordinary odyssey, both in the real world and inside his own mind. He found the courage to face his past and question his belief system. And in doing so, he discovered that the cold, indifferent universe he had lived in for so long was nothing more than his own projection, and that he had the power to change it.

Mesmerized by my father's words and wisdom, I wanted to share his healing journey with a wider audience. But because my father's writing was primarily motivated by his desire to communicate his philosophy, he'd skipped over full decades of his life, leaving me with more questions than answers. I barely knew anything about his past, not even how many siblings he'd had. So much of his history was the history of the Holocaust, and he'd always preferred to avoid that subject.

I spent years researching and writing the missing parts of my father's story, as well as countless hours sorting through, editing, and reorganizing the existing content. While many of these chapters were written by Mendek from start to finish and my only job was editing, I created most of them like a patchwork quilt—carefully sewing together small pieces of copy and information gathered from many diverse sources to form a cohesive whole.

To tell my father's story from his perspective in his voice, I had to look at the world through his eyes—emotionally, spiritually, and intellectually—which meant always holding him close. When I felt his energy land on the page, I knew what I had written was on target.

Turning my father's life story and writings into this book has been a new chapter in our father–daughter relationship, another chance to work together to create something wonderful that neither of us could have accomplished on our own.

When I began my research and needed to learn about my father's early life, my aunt Bronia became my guide. As the only other immediate family member to have survived the war, Bronia was the sole person who could tell me about the grandparents I'd never known and the aunts, uncles, and cousins I would never meet. Thanks to Bronia, I was able to piece together parts of my father's story that he had never shared with me or anyone else.

Much of the new content for this book came from audio and video interviews with my dad that my sister had the foresight to record, interviews my kids conducted with him for school projects when they were young, and interviews I conducted with my mother, sister, family members, and old friends. I also used information gathered from letters our extended family had saved, documents I obtained from the International Tracing Service in Germany, and online research in both the United States and Poland.

Over the years, more and more of my dad's writings would magically appear on my desk or on a shelf that I was sure I had searched before. At times it felt as though he was guiding the process from the other side.

Initially, I thought I was doing my father a favor by fulfilling his wish to share his philosophy with the world. It turned out that he was the one sharing gifts with me. As if reaching out his hand from another dimension to grasp mine, my father is patiently taking me on a transformative journey that's helping me learn how to give up suffering and live a truly joyous life.

Before, I couldn't reconcile my good life with the annihilation of my family, or the torture and humiliation they'd experienced during the Holocaust. The war still lived inside me, as if I had a taproot connecting me to a horror so big I could neither bear to look at it nor ever break free. Following my father's footsteps, I am finally learning how to find peace.

This book also compelled me to reach out to my Orthodox Jewish relatives, the majority of whom I'd never even known existed. Now I have a large and wonderful network of extended family, as well as a rich history that predates the unimaginable cruelty and destruction my predecessors experienced during World War II.

—⁓—

My father's deepest intention was to turn away from darkness and toward the light—to constantly embrace all that is beautiful. He refused to let the enormous trauma of his early life define him or limit his peace and joy in any way. Despite the unfathomable atrocities he was forced to endure, Mendek found his way back to love.

It was my father's greatest hope that his story would inspire others to embark on their own healing journeys. His roadmap to happiness has become an essential part of my own. It is my greatest honor to share it with you.

—Myra Goodman, 2019

MENDEK'S PROLOGUE

As children in Poland, we were told that just before we were born, our guardian angels snapped their fingers under our noses so that we would forget everything we had ever known. This is how we forgot about love. The reason for our being here on earth is to rediscover love all over again.

The journey of my life has been one of coming home to love. Throughout the many decades I was striving to understand the human condition and live a happier life, deep down what I really wanted was to reconnect with a different reality deep inside me—a reality whose foundation was love.

I searched for love as someone else might search for buried treasure, with everything I had in me, every day of my life. And I was surely rewarded. Love has transformed my inner landscape, so that now I have only to look within myself to find satisfaction and the source of all that is good in life. My inner splendor dazzles me.

But it wasn't always this way. For a substantial part of my life, I was unable to find relief from my mental and emotional suffering. I desperately wanted to be happy, but happiness seemed forever out of my reach.

I meekly accepted this painful existence as my fate until I reached middle age, when it seemed as if an alarm clock had suddenly gone off in the recesses of my mind. Something inside of me could no longer accept the status quo. I knew that my life was not what it could or should be, and that something needed to change. I began to revolt against my unacceptable state of existence. I had to find liberation.

I never suspected that lurking in the deepest part of my inner being were my unwanted, feared and forgotten memories—the bottled-up pain and frustration of my entire lifetime, as well as my ancient past. Entering my own psyche felt like penetrating enemy territory. An unyielding jungle of despair and heartbreak was waiting for me. Yet I sensed that I would never be able to find a purpose for life here on earth without looking deep within, so I persevered.

Giving up suffering was the most arduous undertaking of my life. I had no idea what I was up against. Eventually, I discovered that my thoughts—treasured possessions I erroneously interpreted as reality—were at the root of my anguish. I was trapped in my suffering because my instinct for self-preservation extended beyond my physical body and included my state of mind.

It is very difficult when the mind that is trying to solve the problem is the very same mind that created it. My ingrained patterns of thoughts, beliefs, and emotions had a life of their own, and they didn't give way easily. Good or bad, welcome or not, my thoughts came and went without rest. To stop being their helpless victim, I began to explore the uncharted territory of my mind and heart. Before long, this search became my greatest passion.

I did not consciously choose my journey. What was within me simply exerted a pull I could not resist. Some people have the need to climb mountains, others to explore outer space. I turned inward because all other doors were closed to me. I was never sure of my destination until I discovered the power of love.

This is the story of how I was able to break free from the psychological prison I'd lived in since I was a child in a little town in Poland. This is the story of my quest for eternal sunshine.

PART I:

The World I Came From

CHAPTER 1: JAWORZNO

"I believed wholeheartedly that the Messiah would come one day and gather up his children, restoring us to the glory of yesterday. I was waiting expectantly."

I come from a little town in Poland called Jaworzno, which was made up of two very different cultures given to mutual misunderstanding and distrust. Deeply immersed in our religion and way of life, we Jews were the minority. We stood apart from the Christian population not just in our belief system and world outlook, but also in the way we dressed, our language, and our history.

The Poles viewed us as intruders with alien customs, and they treated us with suspicion and contempt. I felt this animosity strongly as a child, and it caused me much grief. It wasn't uncommon for Polish children to scream insults and throw rocks at me on my way to school.

Jaworzno was a coal-mining town, and you could find coal under the earth anywhere you dug. Most of the Jews in Jaworzno were merchants, while most of the Christians worked in one of the five coal mines near town. Mining was hard and dangerous. Mortality rates were high, and every few months, someone was killed.

My family lived right in the middle of the market square, so the long funeral processions always passed by our home on their way to the church. Thousands of mourners dressed in black, accompanied by martial music, followed coffins drawn by horse and buggy.

Jaworzno was a somber place.

—⚏—

The pillar of Jewish religion and culture is the Talmud—the written doctrines and laws that Jews revere the most. Our prayers and dietary laws were all prescribed by the Talmud's rules and customs. This defined my life as a boy. We turned to the Talmud for guidance, wisdom, inspiration, and jurisprudence.

Anyone who was diligent in his learning and well-versed in the study of the Talmud was looked upon with respect, approval, even envy. Becoming a Talmudic scholar was the greatest accomplishment to which a Jewish man could aspire. Those who excelled in wisdom and knowledge occupied places of honor in the synagogue and were considered a blessing to the community.

Preserving our ancient Jewish culture, which we considered divinely dictated, forced us to be an almost self-contained entity. We held on to our unique way of life and were contemptuous of the world around us. This was how we had survived two thousand years of diaspora as a race, culture, and religion. I felt it was only right that God had picked the Jews as his "chosen people," and I was proud of it. I felt superior—better than the gentiles.

The idea of an all-knowing God in heaven who watched over us and guided our destiny was deeply ingrained in my mind. I believed wholeheartedly that the Messiah would come one day and gather up his children, restoring us to the glory of yesterday. I was waiting expectantly. I thought this great miracle would come about soon—that in short order, the dead would rise from their long slumber and triumphantly return home to Jerusalem, the gathering place for all the nations of the world, and anyone who deviated from our religion would be punished. That was why hell was created.

Twice a day—at the break of dawn, and in evening before sunset—all the Jewish men of Jaworzno went to the synagogue to pray. Often, they had to brave bitter cold, snow, and ice to perform their daily rituals. Upon arriving at the synagogue, they sat in their regular places without uttering a word and engrossed themselves in study.

During the long winter nights, after evening prayers were over, the men would stay at the synagogue, our only place for diversion or amusement. We clustered around a tall iron stove, and I, as one of the boys, helped feed the fires. Religion, politics, and philosophy were hotly debated. I learned almost everything I knew from these discussions at the synagogue—from local gossip to international news. I was always extremely curious and listened intently to every word.

On Saturday and during Jewish holidays, every Jewish person in town, from youngest to oldest, was in one of the town's many synagogues, the men and women in different rooms. Not a soul could be found at home.

I was born to Israel and Ida Rubin on September 24, 1924, the second oldest of six children, and the first boy. I had an older sister, Mila, and after me came my brother, Tulek, and then three more sisters: Bronia, Rutka, and Macia.

Jaworzno was my mother's hometown. Her father, Elias Mandelbaum, had sixteen children, but four died in infancy and one died after being kicked by a horse. His four eldest sons eventually settled in other cities, but all five of his daughters and his two youngest sons lived in Jaworzno.

My grandfather Elias was so well off that his substantial holdings were referred to as "The Kingdom of Elias." He had vineyards and was a big producer and supplier of both kosher wine and slivovitz—a type of brandy made from plums. All the Ortho-dox Jews who lived in the Austro-Hungarian Empire bought wine from him. His products were sold as far away as America.

My grandfather had one of the few phones in town. His phone number was 9. Even though he was an Orthodox Jew who lived in an anti-Semitic country, he was elected to the city council and eventually became the town's assessor.

Elias was known far and wide for his charity; it wasn't unusual for him to have forty people around his Sabbath table, many of them beggars and people in need. His wealth, charitable giving, and the substantial dowries he provided for his daughters attracted Talmudic scholars from many different countries in Europe as sons-in-law. My father was one of these scholars.

Elias owned a big building that spanned two blocks right in Jaworzno's market square. My family, as well as the families of two of my aunts and one of my uncles, lived in this building. Our homes were separate, but doors connected them on the inside. We all shared a big courtyard where my cousins and I loved to play.

My family's home was comprised of three rooms: a kitchen; my parents' bedroom, which was very large; and a combined dining and living room, which had two beds, a couch, a folding bed, and the table where we ate our meals. My youngest siblings often slept with our parents in their bedroom. Before the war started, we had a maid who slept in the kitchen. The house had running water and electricity, but the two bathrooms were outside and we shared them with my aunts, uncles, and cousins.

Elias provided each of his children in Jaworzno with a place to live and a storefront. Below our home, on the ground floor, were several family stores, including my father's hardware store. My Aunt Surele and her husband had a tile store, my Aunt Ester Malka had a fabric store, and my uncles Wolf and Shulem had a liquor store, which was also a bar. Jews in our town didn't go to bars to drink, but it was frequented by many of the town's gentiles.

Elias's two oldest daughters shared a two-family house just beyond the church, a couple of blocks from the market square. There, my aunt Brancia and her husband Israel had a wine store, while my aunt Bruncia and her husband Yossele had a popular store that sold many sought-after items, including radios, lamps, bicycles, sewing machines, and cameras.

In addition to being wealthy, Elias was extremely religious. He was the only man in our town with his own synagogue. It was a simple structure he had built in our big courtyard, about the size of one large room. As soon as I could walk, I went there with my father twice a day for morning and evening prayers.

During the *Sukkot* holiday, Jews aren't allowed to eat under a roof because when our people fled Egypt, they wandered in the desert without homes for forty years. In a section of the top floor of his big house, Elias built a roof that opened to the sky just for this occasion. Half of the roof slid over to cover the other half, creating an opening we decorated with branches to make the roof of our *succah*.

This adjustable roof was very exciting to me. During other times of the year, when nobody was looking, I'd sneak upstairs and move the whole thing to the side. I would have been in big trouble if I'd ever been discovered.

My grandfather also made a part of his top floor an apartment reserved only for Passover. The rest of the year, it lay idle. Sometimes I would sneak into this special Passover apartment because it had access to a steep part of the building's roof that I loved to walk on. I had to be careful not to be seen, but it was worth the effort. Up high on that roof, I felt free.

CHAPTER 2: HONOR THY FATHER

"I don't recall ever having a real conversation with my father, but what was not said spoke the loudest."

My father, Israel Rubin, was one of the most well-respected men in Jaworzno. He grew up in Vienna and came from a distinguished line of rabbis and scholars. Studying Torah was in his blood and he could recite it by heart. Through his mother, his lineage traced back to Rabbi Moses Isserles, who lived in the sixteenth century and was one of the most important rabbis in all of Eastern European Jewish history.

My father's mother also had three brothers who were among the most illustrious rabbis in all of Poland. Although their last name was Weidenfeld, they were individually known by the names of the towns where they officiated: The Tshebiner *Rav*, the Dombrover *Rav*, and the Rimalover *Rav*. Once, one of my great-uncles came to visit Jaworzno and it was a huge event for our whole community. Every Jew in town came to see him.

I was named after my paternal grandfather, Yaakov Mendel, a highly esteemed rabbi known as the Toyster *Rav*—the Rabbi of Toyste. He died young, leaving my father to grow up in poverty with his widowed mother. I grew up hearing stories about his greatness.

Although he never went to school and Polish wasn't his first language, my father was self-educated and extremely talented. People in our town who could not read or write came to him to compose letters on their behalf to family, sweethearts, or the authorities.

Nothing would have pleased my father more than to be blessed with a son who excelled in the study of the Talmud and could measure up to his namesake. By the age of five, I was already attending *cheder* full time—the place Jewish boys go to study Hebrew and religion. At seven, I had to go to public school as well, where learning was by rote and the teachers were both dull and harsh. My time was divided between these two schools, leaving me stuck in a classroom from morning until night. I was bored to death.

We spoke Yiddish at home, but my public school classes were taught in Polish. I was self-conscious and couldn't express myself as well as the others at school. There were few Jews, and sometimes I was the only one in the schoolroom. I always felt like a second-class citizen.

Public school was held six days a week, but I missed every Saturday because of *Shabbat*, which put me even further behind. If I wanted to know what happened when I wasn't there, I had to ask a Christian boy, which I hated to do. They treated me with contempt, calling me names like "Dirty Jew" or "Christ killer." The teachers didn't view this as unacceptable behavior. They usually punished the Jewish children more frequently and more harshly.

School was torture for me. Nobody realized that I had dyslexia, which made it very difficult for me to follow along. My mind wandered off in all directions and I had trouble concentrating—except in mathematics, where I was always number one. Every time a question was asked, my hand was up instantaneously, but I failed every other subject miserably. I flunked sixth grade and was unable to finish public school.

Even more traumatic was my poor performance in *cheder*, because that was much more upsetting to my father. It was a generally accepted practice that every Saturday after lunch, all the Jewish fathers would review the previous week's studies with their children. I'd be in a state of tension for days beforehand because I knew I was doing badly. I felt like a disgrace and lived in fear of my father's wrath.

Once, when my father couldn't bear my inadequacies any longer, he lost his temper and went berserk. He beat me for a long time while I lay on the floor. I hated him after that, and my anger and rage made me fear him even more.

Eventually, I learned to run out of the house before the Saturday meal was finished. I knew if I stayed to show my father how poorly I'd performed, he would hit me, but if I ran away, he never punished me. It never occurred to me until much later that he might have felt relieved that he didn't have to.

I don't recall ever having a real conversation with my father, but what was not said spoke the loudest. I perceived him as an intruder in my life, someone out to rob me of my happiness and wellbeing. Our interactions were rooted in anger, hurt, and resentment. I both scorned and feared my father. Mostly, I wanted to avoid him.

I worried that God would not be pleased with my attitude and feared his wrath. I had committed a sin by violating one of the Ten Commandments: "Honor thy father and thy mother." The threat of Judgment Day felt like a permanent shackle around my neck; I was unable to break free. The prayers I recited daily in the synagogue—"Thou shall love thy God with all thy mind, with all thy heart, with all thy soul"—added insult to injury. How could I love and trust a vengeful, punishing God?

—⟶—

My father was an extremely versatile man. An engineer at heart, he took great interest in scientific magazines and new inventions as they trickled into Poland from Germany. He was a carpenter, plumber, and electrician all in one, but he hated running his hardware store, and it wasn't as successful as the other ones in town. Money was always tight.

I, on the other hand, loved our store. When I was a little boy of six, I was already banging nails into tables, driving my father crazy. But no matter what I did, my father still wanted my help. He was short-handed, and I was extremely handy and could always figure things out. When someone came to buy a hinge, I jumped up on the table to get what he needed off the wall.

Once, when I was seven, a man came into the store and told my father he'd lost his keys and couldn't get into his house. It just so happened that I'd recently invented a key that could open any lock, so my father pointed at me and said, "Take him." The man thought it was a joke and was insulted, until he saw how well I got the job done.

In truth, I had two relationships with my father. In the store I was helpful, and he appreciated me. But when it came to learning Talmud, my father was disgusted by my failures. I never came close to measuring up to his expectations. Regardless of how much I helped everywhere else, it didn't really count. Learning Talmud was always what mattered most.

CHAPTER 3: MY BROTHER AND SISTERS

"Unlike his sons, my father was proud of his daughters and didn't view them as disappointments."

My parents got married on September 13, 1921, and their first child, Mila, was born in 1923. Everyone loved my sister. Mila was always cheerful, charming, and kind. She brought sunshine wherever she went and was very popular as well as beautiful.

Mila adored books and my parents even allowed her to read love stories, which surprised me. Sometimes our uncle Yossele would let her ride one of the bicycles from his store. I think Mila loved the freedom she felt riding around town on her own. Once, some members of our congregation confronted my father because they thought Mila was having a demoralizing influence on other children by riding a bicycle in public, but he never told her to stop.

My younger brother, Tulek, was a handsome and playful boy. But like me, Tulek was a big disappointment for our father—in fact, he performed even worse in school than I did. The biggest difference between the two of us was that Tulek openly rebelled.

He often cut school and no one knew where he spent his time. Sometimes he didn't even come home in time for dinner.

While I was generally a quiet, mild-mannered boy, Tulek was often stubborn and a troublemaker. He especially liked to aggravate our sister Bronia. He would often steal her allowance and threaten to break her toys.

Being a few years younger than me, Tulek had to wear my hand-me-down clothes. Unfortunately for both of us, the tailor my mother sent me to most often wasn't very good at his job. It wasn't unusual for him to make one leg of my pants, or one arm of my jacket, longer than the other one. I would have to wear it that way until I outgrew it, and this used to bother me a lot. After me, Tulek would have to wear it for another couple of years. He must have hated it too, but neither of us ever said a thing.

There was a good tailor in town that I loved to go to because he and his family were always kind and cheerful. Unfortunately, my mother only sent me to him occasionally. I don't know if this was because the good tailor was more expensive or because the bad tailor was poor and she gave him her business out of kindness. Maybe it was some of both.

Life seemed easier for my sisters. They attended both public school and Hebrew school, but their days were shorter and they didn't have to go to synagogue after their lessons, so they had much more free time. They often played hopscotch in our court-yard, and sometimes they went to the movies. Our father even built them a dollhouse with miniature furniture.

My sisters' clothing was similar to that of our Polish neigh-bors, so they didn't stand out as targets for anti-Semitism—not like us boys. With our side locks (called *peyos*), skullcaps, and long black coats, we had no chance of fitting in.

Mila's clothes were custom-made by a seamstress to match photos in Parisian magazines, so she always dressed in the latest fashions. Bronia adored Mila above all else and followed her everywhere.

Unlike his sons, my father was proud of his daughters and didn't view them as disappointments. Although he didn't say it aloud for fear of spoiling her, he was very pleased with Bronia's report cards from school. She was a smart girl who met all of his expectations.

Rutka was born two years after Bronia. She was a happy little girl who was always playful and unafraid. When the streets were icy in the winter, she would get a running start and then slide full speed on her feet.

My youngest sister was a sweet, pretty baby named Hana Macia, but we all just called her Macia. My father made her a hobbyhorse and frequently extolled her virtues, but this wasn't surprising, because he thought all of his children were extra special when they were born. There were days when my father would play with one of his babies for hours, but as each of us got older, this stopped completely. My father only expressed his love to us when we were very young.

CHAPTER 4: A LOVING MOTHER

"I don't remember my mother ever raising her voice or doing or saying anything to hurt my feelings."

My mother, Ida Rubin, was very devout—perhaps even more so than my father—but she was never fanatical or dogmatic in her beliefs. Her trust in God came from an abiding faith and love, rather than from fear or obligation. She never demanded that her children follow her brand of religion.

Her siblings called her *"advokat,"* which means lawyer, and often came to her for advice because she was very wise. Kind through and through, she was one of the most selfless people I've ever met. She would often get up very early in the morning to deliver food and other supplies to those in need, making sure to remain anonymous so the recipients wouldn't feel embarrassed by accepting charity. She volunteered to take care of a sick aunt who was a widow without children, and was at her beck and call day and night.

I don't remember my mother ever raising her voice or doing or saying anything to hurt my feelings. I'm sure she worried about how badly I performed in school, but not once in my life was she ever impatient or angry with me. In fact, I can't recall a single time when she criticized any of her children.

The central focus of my mother's life was having a strong relationship with God and being a good wife and mother. As an Orthodox woman, one of her most important responsibilities was preparing our home for the weekly celebration of the Sabbath. She would prepare special food, like home-baked challah, chopped liver, *gribenes* (chicken fat with fried onions), and *chulent* (a stew made out of meat, potatoes, beans, and barley). The *chulent* would simmer throughout the night so we could have a hot lunch, since we weren't allowed to touch electrical switches from sundown Friday until sundown Saturday.

Before *Shabbat*, the men went to immerse themselves in the *mikvah*—a communal purification bath near our town's biggest synagogue. Boys my age weren't required to go, but my brother and I went along to bathe in preparation for Sabbath. My mother and sisters took turns washing in a big, round wooden tub in the kitchen at home.

All of us dressed in our best clothes for *Shabbat*. My father wore a white shirt with a tie, a long black silk coat, and a hat trimmed with mink. My mother wore a special white apron, and brought out our white tablecloths, best china, and heavy silverware.

Each Friday evening before we ate dinner, my father sang *Aishes Chayil* to my mother—the traditional *Shabbat* song in praise of Jewish women. I loved seeing my mother's face grow soft and radiant as my father honored her in this way. Although every Orthodox man sings the same song to his wife, the lyrics seemed to be written just for her, especially the line, "She opens her mouth with wisdom and a lesson of kindness is on her tongue." That was my mother.

—◊◊◊—

Another of my mother's main duties was getting our household ready for the Jewish holidays. My favorites were Passover and Sukkot. They both lasted eight days and everything was special. Though the boys still had to attend public school, we didn't have to go to *cheder*. Every Jew in town went to the synagogue twice a day for a long time, and people were in better moods.

Passover was different from the rest of the year because Jewish law mandated that not one crumb of leavened food be in the house. My mother had to check every pocket in all of our clothes for crumbs and beat all the carpets with brooms. Each of my father's heavy Talmud books had to be taken out to the long veranda so the pages could be checked. Every pot and pan, as well as all the dishes and silverware, had to be stored away, replaced with those used only for Passover. Bread wasn't allowed. The only food made from flour we could eat was *matzo*.

My mother cooked all my favorite Passover foods: chicken soup, beet borscht, beef, chicken, fish, goose, egg omelets, latkes, egg noodles, stewed pears, blueberries, rhubarb with strawberries, cakes made from potato and nut flours. It was a feast, and I got to have big portions of whatever I wanted. It was also the time of year we got new clothes.

Another reason I couldn't wait for Passover was that I got to go to the place where they made matzo. The matzo was round and rolled out by hand. They let the older kids roll it because otherwise they would have had to hire people. I loved the rolling. Sometimes they let me put the matzo in the oven using a long stick with a circle on the end, and later take it out when it was done.

By far, the most festive of all the occasions were weddings. They were great celebrations not to be missed, a time when people set their troubles aside. Luckily, there were plenty of weddings to attend, because I had well over forty cousins in Jaworzno.

I loved music, and weddings were my only opportunity to hear musicians perform my favorite songs. I also enjoyed watching the men sing, dance, and have a great time.

My mother loved music too. Her biggest delight was dancing, and weddings were her only opportunity. She enthusiastically taught my older sister Mila and our cousins all they needed to know to dance with confidence and grace.

During weddings, men and women occupied different rooms and weren't supposed to mingle, but those restrictions did not apply to children. As a child, I had the freedom to shuttle back and forth. When a husband and wife wanted to communicate with each other, I was often the one that carried the messages. When my services were needed, I felt very important.

The highlight of the wedding came toward the end of the evening when the men and women finally came together. The music blasted while the bride and groom danced as a couple, holding hands. Then the bride danced with her father, followed by the father of the groom, holding on to opposite ends of a handkerchief. The festivities went on for a long time, with people happily clapping and dancing.

Those who were more affluent hired a *badchen* to add spice to the festivities. A *badchen* was a special breed of person: a master of ceremonies, a comedian, a storyteller, and a preacher all in one. This versatile entertainer usually divided his time between the men and the women. A good *badchen* was considered a blessing. Even weeks later, people would still talk about the event.

A *badchen*'s greatest virtuosity became evident in the women's section just before the wedding ceremony. His talent manifested in the way he managed to manipulate emotions to such a high pitch that everyone broke down in tears. Right before the official blessings were recited, the *badchen* would give his command performance. He would stand on a chair, facing the bride, her mother, and her closest female family members. Everyone was watching, and it was so quiet you could hear a pin drop. I had to stand on a chair so I could see.

In poetic language, the *badchen* would describe the tremendous responsibilities, hardships, and heartaches awaiting the bride as she embarked on this great adventure of becoming a wife and mother. He described her holy duty to raise Jewish children, the pains and tribulations of bringing them up, the sleepless nights she'd have to endure. As he spoke, I watched the mothers in the room with interest and sadness. They nodded their heads in agreement and sobbed bitterly. They knew the life awaiting their daughters was hard, and their hearts went out to them.

Most of the boys preferred being with the men, but I liked staying with the women better.

When it was time for the dancing to begin, my mother was always the one in charge. Most of the dances were similar to folk dances, and my mother gave orders left and right, directing the operation like a sergeant major.

Was this the same person I knew to be my mother? Just that thought scared me a little. At home, my mother was always busy and worn out from bringing up six children. But at weddings I saw her undergo an amazing metamorphosis—she came alive and was jubilant and tireless.

Somehow, she always managed to create electricity in the air, ensuring that everyone had a great time. I don't remember an occasion when people were as joyous as they were at weddings, myself included.

But soon these good times would come to an end.

CHAPTER 5: TURNING OF
THE TIDES

"Hatred, violence, and round-ups made our lives a terrifying nightmare that never ended."

When I was nine, my grandfather Elias died. The town of Jaworzno honored his passing by flying a black flag over city hall.

My grandfather's death coincided with Hitler's rise to power. Soon, Hitler's Germany became the nightmare of my childhood. Anti-Semitism intensified in Poland, fueled by terrible propaganda from Germany portraying Jews as devious, contaminated, and power-hungry. Every problem was blamed on us, and Christians started boycotting our stores. Some carried placards that said, "Don't buy from Jews!" We were surrounded by hatred, and my family faced increasing financial hardship.

For years prior to the outbreak of World War II, Hitler was the main topic of conversation everywhere. In the synagogue, the men debated issues of war and peace with great passion. It seemed like they knew everything, including the exact words Hitler and

Mussolini said to each other when the two met. These conversations upset me terribly. The mere mention of the German army triggered intense feelings of horror and despair. In my mind, Hitler was both the most wicked and the most powerful man on earth. He was even mightier than God.

—∿—

I became a teenager as Hitler stoked the flames of hatred into an inferno. The Nazis and their collaborators ruled through terror and violence.

Germany began its invasion of Poland on September 1, 1939. Because we lived so close to the German border, our town was one of the first to be occupied. Shortly after, some German soldiers came into our hardware store and forced my father and me into the basement at gunpoint, beating us as we went. They made us face a wall and ordered my father to stand with his hands in the air. They laughed as they told him they were going to shoot him in the back. Although the soldiers eventually left without firing their weapons, my father, who had always been a pillar of strength and composure, was so shaken that he refused to ever set foot in our store again.

Prohibitions against Jews started right after the occupation, and new ones were constantly added. We had to mark ourselves by wearing Jewish stars. At first it was a blue Star of David on a white band on our arms, and then it became a yellow patch in the shape of the star with the word "Jude" on it. This had to be sewn onto both the front and back of all of our clothing.

The men had to change hats and cut off their *peyos*. Even though I had never cut hair before, I was put in charge of going from house to house to do the cutting. I think it must have seemed natural to give me the job, because very often when something needed to be fixed, I was the one called in. I was the only boy who was asked to help the grownups when they were building hiding places.

When I showed up with my scissors, many families panicked. Some of them covered their *peyos* with their hands to stop me from cutting them off. They would rather take a risk and attempt to hide their *peyos* under a hat.

Jews were perpetually under the watchful eyes of the Polish police. Our mail was censored, all travel forbidden, and we weren't allowed to walk on certain streets. Customers stopped patronizing Jewish stores, and suppliers from other towns would no longer sell to us.

Public humiliations were encouraged and commonplace. As people ridiculed us with great enthusiasm, we grew increasingly frightened and filled with shame. It was impossible to feel any optimism about our future. Everything we saw, and all the news we heard, confirmed the hopelessness of our fate.

By the end of 1940, all our valuables had been confiscated and our businesses seized. Men caught in the streets were taken for forced labor. It was illegal to meet in groups, so every time we assembled a *minyan*—the quorum of ten Jewish men required to recite certain prayers—we were breaking the law. It didn't stop the men from going to the synagogue, but every time we did, we risked our lives.

To survive, we were constantly forced to do things that were illegal. The only way my family could get enough to eat was to smuggle out some textiles my aunt had hidden before her store was taken and trade them with a Christian grocer for food. It was decided that my nine-year-old sister Bronia would make the best smuggler. She was small, fast, and could pass as a Christian. My mother had to send her young daughter into extreme danger or let the entire family starve.

The Germans forced me to work in a coal mine. I had to leave very early in the morning, while the rest of my family was still asleep. Because the only grain we could get during the war wasn't milled and took hours to cook, I would eat radishes for breakfast. When I came home after a long day of hard labor, I'd have this gruel for dinner, even though the husks scratched my throat each time I swallowed. None of my siblings were willing to eat it, but I never complained.

When I wasn't working, I'd join Mila and Tulek in the German lessons given by our father. Tulek had no interest in learning the language, which didn't please our father, but I figured it could only come in handy and I welcomed the distraction. Schools were shut down and the atmosphere wasn't one that encouraged play.

Except for the summer months, our house was always freezing. The big tile heater was breaking apart, but it didn't matter because we didn't have coal to heat our house. My mother had health problems and was in constant pain.

In February of 1942, my uncle Yossele's two youngest daughters were taken away to a slave labor concentration camp. My uncle Yossele was my favorite person growing up, and this tragedy affected me greatly. I knew it was only a matter of time before we would all get deported to an unknown destination.

Every day, I lived with the taste of fear in my mouth. My heart beat to the rhythm of terror.

CHAPTER 6: THE WALK

"Birds were singing in celebration of the season, announcing the eternal cycle of renewal. I did not want to die."

One day, while I was working at the coal mine, a commotion nearby caught my attention. A few hundred yards from where I was standing, I saw some workers huddled together, agitated. Their eyes were directed toward the highway just outside the confines of the mine.

I stopped loading coal into a railroad car and stood sideways between the cars to see what was going on. A group of two hundred Jewish men and women of all ages were walking on the open highway leading to the next town. Gazing at the scene in front of me, I was overwhelmed with dread.

The people were walking slowly, in total silence, escorted by German soldiers carrying machine guns. Among the many walkers were the very old and the very young. Infants were being carried in their mothers' arms. Little boys and girls were staying close to their parents. One man was limping and could only walk with a cane.

I watched from the rear since they had already passed by. If it had been five or ten minutes earlier, I would have seen their faces.

I had been working right next to the fence, but hadn't known to look. Now, I was so petrified I couldn't move.

My worst fears were coming to pass. For months, we'd been hearing disturbing news about the Nazis targeting one city after another for evacuation of all the Jewish inhabitants. We lived in dread, not knowing when our turn would come.

Jews were being rounded up and deported by trainloads. None of us knew to what destination, but there were all kinds of rumors. The most prevalent one was that the Jews were being shipped toward the eastern borders of Poland or Russia. The Germans managed to keep the real destination a secret. Perhaps no one really wanted to find out. In my heart, though, I knew their destination was death. Perhaps everyone knew, but we never talked about it.

I later learned that these Jews had been on their way to Auschwitz. It was only fifteen miles away, but at the time, we had no idea it existed, or that the systematic extermination of all the Jewish people in Poland had begun.

—⟋⟍—

Our shift ended at two o'clock in the afternoon that day, but we were too terrified to go home. Only in the evening, after word came that the coast was clear, did we dare leave our place of work. When I finally got back to Jaworzno, I was comforted to learn that none of my immediate family had been among the marchers.

Watching that walk has haunted me my entire life. It evoked feelings of rage, helplessness, and humiliation that I desperately wanted to forget. Instead of focusing my rage outward toward the perpetrators, I turned it inward.

In the years to come, my mind went over this episode again and again, pondering the apparent calm of these people in their encounter with destiny. The pace of the march was relaxed, as though it were an everyday event. They looked like people on their way to a picnic. Even the German guards seemed relaxed, their machine guns hung loosely on their shoulders. They knew nobody was going to run away.

It was the stillness of the marchers that felt so terrifying and unbelievable. Even the children were silent. None of them cried. It was as if they, too, sensed the gravity and inevitability of the situation, and quietly submitted to their fate.

Poland often had delightful weather that time of year, and it had been especially beautiful on that particular day. The land seemed overjoyed with the coming of spring. The sun had been warming up the ground for a few weeks, melting the snow and causing the earth to come alive and reawaken from slumber after the long, cold winter. The trees and bushes were in full bloom, perfuming the air. The deep blue sky extended as far as my eyes could see, embracing the world around me. Birds were singing in celebration of the season, announcing the eternal cycle of renewal. I did not want to die.

As I stood there frozen, watching these people moving into the shadows toward disaster, I knew that their hours and days were numbered. They would never see another springtime in its glory. I feared my turn was next. I felt my selfishness deeply. I wanted to survive at all costs.

A few weeks later, our town's Jewish council was told that the Jews had to deliver forty people to the labor camps. Every family had to pick one person to go. No one was expected to return alive. My parents had to make this choice. Because I wanted to save them from having to choose, I volunteered.

In May of 1942, at seventeen, I found myself on my way to a slave labor concentration camp in Germany. I was part of a group of forty teenagers and young men from my hometown that had been forcibly separated from our families and led to the railroad station. Escorted by armed guards, we were taken to a depot in another town from which Jewish inmates were distributed to labor camps in Germany.

On my way to the station, I was surprised to see my parents standing on one of the side streets. I passed them in silence. A few moments later, I turned around and our eyes met again. I felt their love and concern for me. When I was already quite some distance away, they were still standing there. It was the last time I ever saw them.

The truth is, I was glad to be leaving. I sensed in my bones that going to a slave labor camp might be my only chance of survival. We still had not heard of Auschwitz, but I had a premonition that my parents, and most of the people in my hometown, would be killed off before this war was over. When I looked at my parents' faces, I felt guilty for wanting to live. My selfishness was a constant weight upon me during those three long years.

It turned out that I was right—leaving is what made it possible for me to survive. But of the forty men and teenagers that left Jaworzno that day, I was the only one still alive after the war. All the others died from starvation and hard labor.

Several months after I was taken, my parents must have walked that very same road, heading to their deaths in Auschwitz. Except for a handful of survivors, the Jewish population in my hometown was completely decimated.

CHAPTER 7: SURVIVAL MACHINE

"The Nazis' aim was to starve us to death while we performed heavy or treacherous labor."

I have never talked about the worst atrocities I experienced during my three years in seven different slave labor concentration camps. My imagination could never have created a hell like the one I endured. The teenage boy I had once been was quickly transformed into a survival machine.

Staying alive required enormous effort every day. I always had to keep my eye on the guards and never be caught idling. If you were beaten for not working hard, you usually couldn't recover. People sometimes stole from each other, but if you were suspected of stealing, your life was over. I never stole a thing.

Our rations were never meant to be enough to keep us alive. We only received food once a day, when we came back from work, and it was almost always soup. Everyone had a cup, and if you were really lucky, they filled it up with heavy stuff, like potatoes. Other times, you only got liquid. I figured out the best time to get in line to increase my odds of getting the most food—not in the beginning, because the good stuff was still on the bottom, and not in the end, because by then it was gone. My strategy was common sense, but most people were too hungry to wait.

After the soup, there was a sack where you could get drinking water. People stood in line for it, often waiting for hours to get a sip. Even though I was thirsty, the energy it took to stand for so long wasn't worth it. Instead, I went back to the barracks to lie down. I knew that to survive I had to always conserve my energy. Resting made the most sense.

While I was starving, I comforted myself by fantasizing about eating huge amounts of potatoes. I imagined them prepared in different ways: fried, baked, mashed with butter. It never occurred to me to wish for fancier food. We got small amounts of potatoes as part of our rations, and an abundance of them was the biggest luxury I could imagine. Just the thought of having as many potatoes as I wanted was heaven on earth.

The winters in Poland were freezing. We were given just one thin blanket apiece to keep us warm at night in the barracks. I kept warmer than the others because I figured out how to roll up in the blanket so I'd be covered with two to three layers, instead of just one. I went to the farthest end of the narrow bunk, rolled over, then pushed myself back to the end over and over again. If I hadn't figured this out, I might not have survived.

If we became sick or unable to work, that was the end. There were many times that I came close to dying, but I got lucky. I had diarrhea once, which was almost always a death sentence. Somehow, my cousin Stanley found out I was sick and got someone to bring me a piece of charcoal to eat. That stopped the diarrhea, and probably saved my life.

Another time, I was sick when we were supposed to move to a new camp because ours was being liquidated. There was no way I could have made the walk, but a storm came in the night before, postponing the transfer. Then it was postponed again for a reason I never knew. When it was finally time to go, I had recovered enough to make the trip. Many prisoners never survived the exertion of those transfers.

The Nazis' goal was to starve us to death while we performed heavy or treacherous labor. At my first labor camp, there were ten different places where prisoners worked. It was a large complex that used a tremendous amount of coal, and my job was to load the coal onto trains. It was backbreaking work, and I didn't know how long I'd have the strength to continue. Still, it was better than other jobs that were less strenuous but far more dangerous, like working with toxic chemicals. The inmates who did that kind of work died very quickly.

I'd been at that camp for four months when my sister Mila saved my life. During the final roundup in Jaworzno, Mila and my younger sisters had escaped to the neighboring town of Sosnowiec. During the short time we were allowed to write letters, I mentioned that the *kapo* at my labor camp was the son of a man we had once done business with at our hardware store, and that he was from Sosnowiec.

Kapos were Jews put in charge of the other prisoners, and they were the ones who assigned the jobs. These men were given adequate food and didn't have to do heavy labor. Compared to us, they lived like kings. They were notorious for their cruelty.

As soon as my sisters arrived in Sosnowiec, Mila began searching for my *kapo*'s parents. Eventually she located them, went to their home, and begged them to ask their son to help me. She gave them her one valuable possession—a beautiful hand-knit sweater—hoping the gift would encourage them to follow through.

The *kapo*'s parents must have kept their word and asked him to take care of me, because he took me out of the really hard job and gave me an easier one—feeding the furnaces with coal, removing the ash, loading it onto wagons, and dumping it off the side of a hill.

During the winter, thirty of us were needed for this job, but when summertime came, it only required one person. They picked me because I was the handiest. I had figured out how to move the full wagons by myself by placing the rails ahead of the wagon piece by piece, and I could do it quickly.

Not only was I able to keep the best job while the others were out doing heavy shoveling all day, I got very lucky working there. Some inmates had found a stash of raw potatoes but had no way to cook them. They gave the potatoes to me and I cooked them in the hot ashes. As payment, I received one potato for every three that I cooked.

The best jobs could keep you alive. If my sister hadn't arranged for me to be given an easier one, I wouldn't have survived.

CHAPTER 8: THE FINAL
DAYS OF WAR

"The most powerful military on earth was disintegrating. Their aura of invincibility was gone."

The labor camp I was in during the spring of 1945 was located only a few blocks from the main road that ran through Bavaria, Germany. Night and day, for weeks on end, we listened to the rumbling of tanks and other armored vehicles on the move. The Russians were now on German soil, in pursuit of their bitter enemy.

We could tell the Russian armies were closing in. From inside our barracks, we heard the sounds of battle getting closer and louder. We silently celebrated the artillery cannons blasting away. Sometimes I couldn't sleep for hours, I was so excited.

Our imprisonment would soon come to an end, and we wondered what fate would ultimately befall us. We feared that our freedom would be snatched away at the last minute, our deaths the revenge of the defeated people guarding the prison camp.

After what seemed like eternity, we could see and hear the German armies in retreat. Even though all the factories had ceased working and the nearby town was increasingly deserted, the German authorities in charge of our camp pretended that nothing had changed. Every day, under guard, we were sent out to work as usual. But on the job, there was a great silence. Everything was at a standstill. You could feel the tension in the air.

Each morning on our way to work, and every evening when we returned to the camp, we witnessed an exodus of major proportions. We became spectators of the high drama playing out on the open highway. Families, large and small, were on the move. Oxcarts and wagons were loaded to the brim with personal belongings. Children sat on top of the wagons playing with toys, oblivious to the drama unfolding all around them. Some people rode bicycles, but many walked, carrying bundles on their backs. They were not sure where they were going or how long it would take to get there.

As the Russian armies closed in, the roads became increasingly jammed, teeming with masses of humanity on the run. Entire towns and villages took to the roads, heading west. This included the civilians who had left their homes to join the German army in a desperate effort to flee for safety from the invading armies of the East.

The roads were so crowded that everything moved at a snail's pace. The demoralized German army was often caught in this traffic jam. Some of the German soldiers rode in trucks, tanks, or armored vehicles, while the infantry was on foot. The officers were chauffeured in cars or three-seated motorcycles.

Many of the German soldiers were teenagers. In their worn-out uniforms, they did not appear as ominous as they had when I'd first encountered them at the start of the war. They looked exhausted and harassed, no longer a conquering army that no one could stop. The most powerful military on earth was disintegrating. Their aura of invincibility was gone.

Now that I was witnessing their downfall, I rejoiced at their defeat. Sometimes I feared that I would burst out laughing, and that would be my end. I wanted to pinch myself, overcome as I was with disbelief that such a miracle could happen. Germany had really lost the war! For years, I had been conditioned to believe in the unassailable might of Hitler's armies. The inhabitants of all their conquered territories had been terrified of them. But now they had been beaten.

—⁂—

On our way to work in the morning, we walked in the opposite direction of the retreating German army. In the evenings, on our way back to the camp, we walked in the same direction, side by side.

The German army had once loomed ten feet tall in my imagination—dragon-like creatures capable of destroying the world. Ever since they'd invaded my hometown, I hadn't dared to look at their faces. But now, on those morning walks, I couldn't help but make eye contact with the soldiers walking toward me.

In the beginning, it felt like I was watching people from another planet—an alien force determined to destroy me and my people. Looking directly at my executioners was like staring hell right in the face. Yet in spite of my nervousness, my eyes remained glued to their faces. I couldn't help myself. When they looked at me, I quickly glanced away. I needed to be cautious and I was still afraid.

After a while, my fears subsided a little and I began to scrutinize the soldiers as if seeing them for the first time. I watched their faces and observed their manners—the way they walked and talked, how they smoked their cigarettes, the kind of weapons and ammunition they carried. I was overwhelmed with curiosity.

After several days, as my fear continued to lessen, in my mind I dared them to make eye contact with me. Although this scared me, I began to notice that the German soldiers were human beings after all. They had eyes, mouths, hands, and feet. They walked and talked like everyone else. *They might even have feelings like other people*, I thought, though that was a revelation I found hard to believe.

Some were my age, with kind and sensitive eyes. It actually seemed possible that they could be nice. Perhaps, in another situation, we could have been friends. As I examined them, I stopped seeing them as monsters, and wondered why that was the case. As my fear and hatred began to lighten, I felt guilty. I thought I was betraying my people. This, in turn, made me feel sad and lonely, but I didn't know why.

Even though I had witnessed unspeakable brutality, something in me did not want to believe that it was true. There was a part of me that found it too painful to accept the cruelty and savagery of the human race. How could these men in front of me—even those who seemed kind—kill so easily?

Perhaps, I mused, *I am no different than these German soldiers. Perhaps we are all the same. Would I behave like them if I were in their shoes?*

These are questions I still ask myself.

Eventually, as I studied the soldiers on those walks, I began breathing easier. A heavy weight was lifted from my shoulders. The German army had troubles of their own now, so I knew they were less likely to harm me. Yet I could not fully rejoice. I was still under guard and did not know what the future would bring.

For the first time in three years of subhuman existence, I was coming in contact with people outside the concentration camps. The masses of people—old and young, women and children—evoked a feeling of kinship with the human race. I began to feel a flicker of humanity reawakening within me.

One evening, as we were walking on the crowded road on our way back to camp, one man's face stood out among the multitude. We were heading in the same direction as the traffic, but at a faster pace, and we were catching up to him. He must have felt our gaze upon him because he slowed in the hope of creating some distance between us. He was not looking at us, but many of us were looking at him.

We Jewish prisoners knew he was a Jew, and he knew that we knew. Terror was written on his face. He was hiding his identity and pretended to ignore us out of fear that the German guards would discover who he was. It did him no good. One of the wardens noticed our interest in him, and he was apprehended. He was brought to our camp, where he was shot the same evening.

That man must have realized that his hours were numbered, because his face revealed a person who knew he was doomed. He was probably an escapee from another camp, or maybe he'd been living in hiding. When I first saw him on the road walking free, I got very excited. For a short time, he was a symbol of freedom. I couldn't believe that I was about to become a free man.

Perhaps if I hadn't looked at him, his life could have been saved. I blamed myself for his death for a long time. People dying meant almost nothing to me during my three years in the concentration camps—the deaths were so frequent and so numerous that I became numb to them—but this case stood out from the others. This episode kept reappearing before my eyes, always evoking a unique response—a feeling of existential isolation. I was utterly alone in the world, desolate and forlorn.

CHAPTER 9: LIBERATION

"You could almost touch death in the air. Virtually every person I had ever known—the only life I had ever known— had been destroyed."

At the break of dawn on May 5, 1945, when the sun was still hiding behind the horizon and most people were still deep asleep, I woke up to a clatter. Agitation was in the air. From far away, I heard a faint voice saying, "They are gone."

I dressed quickly and walked out of the barracks. The place was deserted. I turned the corner toward the main gates where guards were usually posted. It was true. One of the gates was wide open. The Germans had pulled out in the middle of the night.

Cautiously, I made my way to the gates, constantly looking over my shoulder. I hesitated for a while. Then, with a beating heart, I walked out into the open country. Breathing heavily, I realized that I had survived the war.

For a few minutes, it seemed like a fairy tale, but my mood quickly changed. I was relieved it was over, but I had no urge to sing and dance, as I had expected I would if this moment ever came.

As I looked around, there was only a barren field with a few old neglected trees and the deep, depressing silence of dawn. It felt like the residue of a bad dream. Everything was still. I didn't see another soul. Nothing held any attraction for me.

Standing outside of the confines of the camp made me nervous. After a few minutes, I went back to join the others. A bunch of us stood there in striped uniforms, speechless. We didn't know what to do. For many hours, nobody ventured out. Then a Russian officer who spoke Yiddish walked over to tell us that our concentration camp had been liberated by the invading Russian army. He gave us the assurance that the coast was clear.

Outside, the sun was shining, and the blue sky had never been so beautiful. For just a short while, I was elated.

—⁓—

Months later, when the war ended, I went back to my hometown with two of my cousins who had also managed to survive. Before the war, Jaworzno had a population of twenty-four thousand, two thousand of whom were Jews. What we found was a ghost town.

You could almost touch the death in the air. Virtually every person I had ever known—the only life I'd ever known—had been destroyed. Only one Jewish family was still living there, a family from a different part of town than ours. If not for them, we wouldn't have had a place to sleep or food to eat.

An entire community rich in tradition, culture, and prayer, had been wiped out. The voices from the synagogues and the laughter of children in our extended family's backyard would never be heard again. There was a heavy silence everywhere.

I was overtaken by deep anxiety, but other than that, I didn't feel a thing. I couldn't wait to get out of there. There was nothing for me to do but move on.

I went back to the part of Germany that was under American occupation and idled away the hours, with nothing to do and without too much on my mind. Satisfied to live on the food rations and supplies handed out freely to former concentration camp inmates, I appreciated my freedom while waiting to emigrate to the United States or Israel. I expected it to take years.

—m—

After living in Germany for a while, I was shocked to find out that my younger sister Bronia was alive. Against all odds, Bronia had managed to live through one-and-a-half years in Auschwitz. I couldn't believe she'd made it. I had been certain that except for a few cousins, everyone in my family had been murdered—my parents, all my siblings, every aunt and uncle.

A cousin of ours discovered that Bronia was alive while looking for survivors on his father's side of the family. He found her in Slovakia, living with a woman named Bozenka who had saved her life in Auschwitz, and he brought her to me in Germany. Through Bronia, I learned what had happened to the rest of my family.

Not long after I was taken, in the summer of 1942, my family had been ordered to report to the local schoolyard. My parents risked reporting with only two of their children, Tulek and Bronia. My father had told Mila to take our youngest sisters, Rutka and Macia, and go to our family's hiding place in my aunt's attic.

After being held all day under the hot sun in the schoolyard, my mother took a risk and told Bronia to try and get away, despite knowing that she might be gunned down before her eyes. Bronia's experience smuggling probably helped her escape unnoticed. She ran to a Christian neighbor's farm, where she hid until dark, and then went to find our sisters.

It was too dangerous for the girls to stay in Jaworzno for even one night. The Nazis were completing their final roundup to make Jaworzno *Judenrein*, "cleansed of Jews," and Nazi guards searching for Jews in hiding surrounded the entire town. My sisters used back roads to flee to Sosnowiec, which had not yet been made *Judenrein*. They had no food or water, just the clothes on their backs and one valuable possession: a beautiful hand-knit sweater Mila grabbed on her way into hiding that she later used to save my life.

In Sosnowiec, my sisters slept outside and begged for food until someone told them that children under twelve could get ration cards and be given shelter. But a few months later, all the Jews in Sosnowiec were forced to relocate into the ghetto. My sisters were assigned one tiny, dilapidated room. Soon after, nine of our close relatives found my sisters and moved in with them, so thirteen people shared that one small space.

Jews weren't allowed to leave the ghetto. When our family began to starve, Bronia had to become a smuggler again. She would sneak out of the ghetto to purchase a live chicken from a neighboring farmer, and then sneak back in, holding it under her shawl. It was a huge risk every time. One noise from the chicken would have alerted the German soldiers and given her away.

My family could never afford to eat the chickens. Instead, they sold them on the black market to get money to buy potatoes and bread, which stretched much farther.

In August of 1943, all the Jews in Sosnowiec were rounded up and packed into cattle cars that took them to Auschwitz. When the train doors opened, German guards with guns, clubs and fierce dogs began screaming, "Out! Out! Quickly! Leave everything behind. Move faster!"

Bronia, Rutka, and Macia were told to go to the line on the left that led directly to the gas chambers. Mila was sent to the line on the right that headed to the forced labor concentration camps. But instead of going where she was told, Bronia ran after Mila.

Immediately upon arrival, my sisters were stripped naked. Male inmates shaved their entire bodies until they were bald, and then their arms were tattooed with prisoner numbers.

Mila and Bronia worked long days on only one bowl of watery soup and a slice of bread made mostly from sawdust. In the barracks, they slept crowded together on wooden planks with just one thin blanket for many women to share, despite the freezing Polish winters. There was no way to get clean, and only one latrine for hundreds of people. Before long, Mila and Bronia became skeletons covered with lice and sores from scratching.

After a few months, Mila came down with typhus and could no longer do heavy labor. She was sent to the *Revier*, the barracks where sick people were housed in terrible conditions without any medical care. Bronia went with her.

Then a day came when all of the sick and dying prisoners were to be collected and sent to the gas chambers. Bozenka—the Jewish nurse in charge of the barracks who had been one of only three prisoners out of a thousand to survive her transport from Slovakia—risked her life to save Bronia. She pretended that Bronia was her sister so that she had a reason to keep her off the list of those being taken away.

Bozenka continued to care for Bronia when she became so sick with typhus that she went into a coma for a long time. Bronia was still terribly ill during the Death March in January 1945. Bozenka carried Bronia whenever she couldn't keep up to prevent her from being shot. After liberation, certain that Bronia was an orphan with no family remaining, Bozenka brought her home to Slovakia and enrolled her in school there. She would have kept Bronia forever if our cousin hadn't found her.

—◆—

Bronia and I had suffered terribly and lost so much that neither of us could put our pain into words, not even to each other. We'd both witnessed unthinkable horrors that could never be erased. The memories of what we'd lost forever were both precious and torturous. Except for each other, everything we loved had been destroyed. Parts of us had been destroyed as well.

We had no idea how difficult it would be to live with what had happened. Bronia felt guilty for being alive. She couldn't stop thinking about Mila or our two baby sisters dying alone in the gas chamber without her there to hold their hands.

Neither of us knew how to move on. We had nothing to look forward to, just anguish and devastation to run away from. Although we'd survived, living without a home or family in a world full of unfathomable cruelty did not feel at all like a triumph.

Mandelbaum Family Tree

* Murdered in the Holocaust

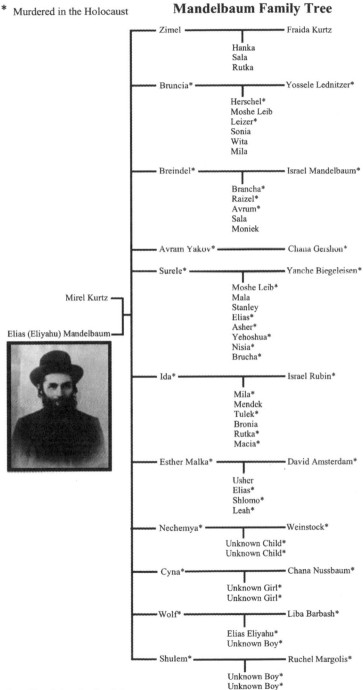

Elias (Eliyahu) Mandelbaum — Mirel Kurtz

- Zimel — Fraida Kurtz
  - Hanka
  - Sala
  - Rutka
- Bruncia* — Yossele Lednitzer*
  - Herschel*
  - Moshe Leib
  - Leizer*
  - Sonia
  - Wita
  - Mila
- Breindel* — Israel Mandelbaum*
  - Brancha*
  - Raizel*
  - Avrum*
  - Sala
  - Moniek
- Avram Yakov* — Chana Gershon*
- Surele* — Yanche Biegeleisen*
  - Moshe Leib*
  - Mala
  - Stanley
  - Elias*
  - Asher*
  - Yehoshua*
  - Nisia*
  - Brucha*
- Ida* — Israel Rubin*
  - Mila*
  - Mendek
  - Tulek*
  - Bronia
  - Rutka*
  - Macia*
- Esther Malka* — David Amsterdam*
  - Usher
  - Elias*
  - Shlomo*
  - Leah*
- Nechemya* — Weinstock*
  - Unknown Child*
  - Unknown Child*
- Cyna* — Chana Nussbaum*
  - Unknown Girl*
  - Unknown Girl*
- Wolf* — Liba Barbash*
  - Elias Eliyahu*
  - Unknown Boy*
- Shulem* — Ruchel Margolis*
  - Unknown Boy*
  - Unknown Boy*

Created from the best of our knowledge, as
no official records have ever been located.

3 million of Poland's 3.3 million Jews were murdered in the Holocaust

Treblinka

Warsaw

Chelmno

Poland

Sobibor

Majdanek

Germany

Belzec

Sosnowiec

Jaworzno

Mielec

Auschwitz

Krakow

Tarnow

Czechoslovakia

Wadowice

Key
✖ Extermination Camp
● City
★ Capital
━ 1939 Borders

North

50 Miles

PART II:

The World I Discovered

CHAPTER 10: A NEW BEGINNING

"I'd heard that the streets of America were paved with gold, but that was not the case."

Just before the war started, my cousin, Simon Geldwerth, immigrated to America from Vienna. Simon was the son of my father's older sister, and Bronia and I had only met him a few times, on the rare occasions when he'd visited our family in Poland.

In 1941, Simon somehow managed to rescue his parents, brother, and sister-in-law from a French concentration camp and bring them to America on what may have been the last boat out of Europe, right before the bombing of Pearl Harbor. After that, there was nothing Simon could do to save the rest of his family members still in Europe, but when the war was over, he tried to track down and help anyone that had survived.

When Simon found out that Bronia and I were alive, he dedicated himself to getting us the necessary papers to come to the United States. Without Simon, we would have been trapped in desolate post-war Europe indefinitely.

On August 22, 1946, when I was twenty-one and Bronia was fifteen, we boarded the Marine Perch, an army liberty liner in Bremerhaven, Germany. Ten days later, on a misty morning at the break of dawn, I was standing on deck in the New York Harbor, staring at a cold, impersonal city of steel and skyscrapers.

All my attention was on the endless caravan of cars speeding rapidly along the West Side Highway toward their appointed destinations, as if the world were running out of time. There had only been two cars in all of Jaworzno, and both were taxis.

Behind me, I felt the welcoming presence of the Statue of Liberty. A symbol of freedom and tolerance, she represented my adopted country, my future. Simon was waiting for us at the pier.

There were many rumors in America at that time that Holocaust survivors could be wild and destructive. Despite these warnings, Simon and his parents took us in. Bronia and I were orphaned and financially dependent on Simon, who worked double shifts at a factory to support us all.

We lived with Simon and his parents—our aunt and uncle, whom we'd never met before—in a small one-bedroom apartment in Brooklyn. The only place for us to sleep was in the hallway, and we knew we were imposing. I lived there for five years, and Bronia for seven, until she got married.

—m—

I'd heard that the streets of America were paved with gold, but that was not the case. My expectations that it would be a Shangri-La did not materialize. I couldn't speak English and had no marketable skills, so it was very hard to find work. I took whatever jobs I could get. One winter there was a huge storm, which proved lucky for me, because I got a lot of work shoveling snow.

Emotionally, I lived a marginal existence, withdrawn and fearing intimacy. The Holocaust had made me cynical, cold, and mostly indifferent to the world around me. I believed that everyone was capable of the brutality I had experienced during the war; it was only a matter of circumstance.

I'd started having nightmares after I was liberated, and they never stopped. I was frequently awakened by a recurring dream of being trapped in an icy cold, barren North—a starved inmate forced to do backbreaking labor all day long and late into the night. Images of a cruel human race and an indifferent universe were etched into my consciousness.

Bronia had troubles as well. I could sense her constant anxiety. She never felt safe and wouldn't leave the house without carrying food with her. She distrusted people in authority and assumed all non-Jews were anti-Semitic. She was no longer able to either laugh or cry.

When we first arrived in America, I thought our problems would soon be over. I felt very enthusiastic about the beliefs and sentiments expressed in the Declaration of Independence: "We hold these truths to be self-evident, that all men are created equal, that they are endowed by their Creator with certain unalienable Rights, that among these are Life, Liberty and the pursuit of Happiness." Yet I felt neither free nor happy, and this frustrated me to no end. I needed a roadmap to happiness, but I couldn't find one.

During those initial years in America, Bronia and I spent much of our time together. We'd go to the movies every week for a double feature, and take the subway to visit our few relatives in New York so we could become acquainted. There is no way we would have found them if Simon hadn't tracked them down for us. In Jaworzno, we'd had so many first cousins that a second cousin was barely considered a relative. Now, second cousins were close relations. The war had changed everything.

Bronia went to the local high school during the day, while I went to night school to get my high school equivalency diploma. It took years to become good English speakers. We made a lot of embarrassing mistakes and were self-conscious about pronouncing words incorrectly.

Bronia had always been very smart. Even though she had just begun learning English and had only been in school through the first grade in Poland, she wanted to take additional classes to finish high school in three years instead of four. For this request to be considered, she had to present her case at a meeting with the school's principal and department heads. Being proud of me and wanting to brag about how handy I was, Bronia told the committee that her brother was very "handicapped," thinking it was a more sophisticated word for "handy." When everyone looked concerned and asked her what was wrong with me, she had to explain her mistake. Nonetheless, she was granted permission to take the extra classes.

It took me a long time to make friends with young men my own age. Simon had managed to get Bronia and me on one of the first boats out of Europe, so we were among the earliest Holocaust survivors to settle in Brooklyn. The bulk of Jewish refugees came a few years later.

Eventually, I started getting together with some of the other unmarried guys living in our neighborhood to take walks and chat. Sometimes we'd go see a movie.

—⁓—

While all the other survivors I knew slowly became very religious again, I never did. My experiences in the concentration camps loosened my bonds with my former life. I breathed a sigh of relief at the realization that I no longer had to deal with my father, God, or religion. I stopped the practices of my Orthodox upbringing, and no longer adhered to Jewish dietary laws.

Nonetheless, my old guilt endured. Every time I ate non-kosher food, I looked over my shoulder to make sure no one was looking. Even though I had rebelled against my parents and culture, there was still an umbilical cord tying me to my past.

I was haunted by images of a vindictive God bent on punishment and retribution—a God who resided in heaven that had nothing better to do than monitor my thoughts, actions, and behavior. As a child, I'd been taught that human beings have a soul that survives the physical body. After we die, we move into the "beyond," where we'll have to give an account of ourselves. The "beyond" was very serious business. I believed that on Judgment Day, I'd face a stern and punishing God, and I'd be in big trouble because I was bad.

All this changed overnight when I learned something that made me realize that my fear was unfounded.

It happened soon after I came to the United States, during night school. One evening, the topic in biology class was evolution, and we were shown both a human and a chicken embryo preserved in bottles. What shocked me was how similar the two embryos looked soon after conception. I could hardly tell them apart. The teacher told us that both embryos could be traced to the early stages of our common evolutionary beginning.

The concept of evolution caught me off guard. Even though I saw the evidence right in front of me, it was so strange that I could hardly believe it at first. All life on this planet—including mammals, fish, trees, and flowers—could trace their roots to the very same source. In certain ways, humans were just like worms.

Back in my hometown, we'd heard rumors that people were descended from monkeys, but no one had believed it. It was heresy. Humans were the children of God, and God had created us in his image. But suddenly, in just a few minutes, my mind changed forever. We did come from monkeys!

Humans were not the children of God, as the Bible said. Rather, we were all part of nature. I further reasoned that if we were not made in God's image, perhaps there was no God. Because we shared a common destiny with all living things, and since it was inconceivable to me that monkeys would be subjected to a Judgment Day after death, why must we be?

In a flash, all my fears vanished. From that day forward, I no longer believed in a God of retribution. As a matter of fact, I didn't believe in God at all. I was doubly liberated. That night, I went to bed happy.

But eventually, I felt much like a branch that had been severed from a tree, its source of life. I ached for a relationship with something greater than myself, that which creates and sustains us all. I had a deep, persistent need to confirm that there was indeed meaning inherent in the human struggle. I thought that to be happy I would have to know for certain that love, forgiveness, and generosity are a legitimate part of this life. I looked around for proof, but had a hard time finding substantial evidence.

CHAPTER 11: KOREA

"It made me wonder if somehow I was meant to survive."

Four years after I arrived in America, the war in Korea broke out and I was drafted into the United States Army. I was inducted on October 4, 1950, and sent to Camp Atterbury in Indiana for basic training.

My family felt this was a great tragedy. They tried to get me released, or at least not sent into combat. My cousin Simon, who was my legal guardian because I was not yet a citizen, petitioned the government, as did Bronia. They cited the Selective Service Act of 1948, which exempted sole surviving sons from induction. Simon and Bronia requested a deferment or reclassification for me because I was the only surviving son from a family that had been slaughtered by the Nazis. But they were told that since both my parents had been killed, the clause did not apply; neither would be alive to mourn the loss of their only son.

Despite my family's distress, I was glad to be in the army. It felt honorable to fight for my new homeland. I wanted to protect the free world and prove my bravery. Also, the army fascinated me— the way it was organized, the strategies it employed, its weaponry.

Being in the military was also the first time I hadn't had to worry about money. Since arriving in America, I'd only been able to find occasional, short-term, low-paying jobs and had to think about every single cent I spent. I'd made a habit of going to automat cafeterias where sandwiches cost twenty-five cents and I could eat crackers and packets of ketchup for free. Now, my salary made it possible for me to save money and send some home, which felt great. I didn't even have to pay postage for the letters I sent to my family.

After three months of basic training, I waited with anxious anticipation to learn where I would be stationed. More than once, I was on the list to be sent to Korea, but each time my orders were recalled at the last minute. Because mortality rates were high in Korea, most soldiers considered this to be a good thing, but for me, it was a disappointment. Uncertainty made me impatient, and I was curious about what life was like in such a faraway country.

Eventually, I was sent to the war zone. The ship that took us there stopped in Tokyo for ten days, and what I saw of Japan fascinated me. When I arrived in Korea, I was stationed ninety miles from Pusan while awaiting my assignment. All the soldiers slept together in big tents, surrounded by mountains and lots of Korean children.

This was a time of great hardship for the Korean people. Their country was divided and at war with itself, one side against the other. Yet despite the upheaval, hunger, and poverty, the atmosphere did not appear to be one of sadness or bitterness. I often saw smiles on people's faces. They seemed relaxed, peaceful, and even joyful. I expected them to be sad and despondent, and wondered why this wasn't the case.

America promises everyone access to happiness, and maybe it's that expectation that backfires. In wartime Korea, almost everyone was poor and many people's needs went unmet, but they did not often appear unhappy. Perhaps it was because they had fewer expectations.

—〰—

When I was first drafted, I was given aptitude tests that revealed my mechanical abilities, so I was trained to be a radio operator. In Korea, even though I'd never driven a car in my life, I was given a vehicle. They showed me the pedals, gave me the keys, and said, "Try it." I had to start driving immediately.

I was assigned to a pair of American officers who worked with the Koreans, right behind the front lines. If contact was needed with the other companies, my job was to communicate with them.

Every Korean regiment had two American officers who served as liaisons to coordinate the war effort. Korean officers weren't allowed to sleep in the same tent as American officers, and as an enlisted man, neither was I. That's how I came to share a tent with the Korean officers and their two houseboys.

Quickly, one of the houseboys, Yu, became my best friend. Yu came from a poor family and didn't have the same advantages as the officers, but despite his lack of education, he was smarter than most of his superiors. He was extremely mechanical and would often take the lead, saying, "Mendek, let's do it this way." He gave me new ideas, which hadn't happened before. Growing up, I'd always been the handiest one. Finally, in Yu, I'd met my match.

While it took other men all day to set up a new camp, Yu and I did it in two hours because we worked so well together. Before he verbalized his idea, I knew it, and before I made a suggestion, he'd already guessed it. Even though we came from completely different worlds and his English was not the best, we had a special kinship. I had never known anybody else who understood me on that level, and we had some very good times on our days off. If Yu and I had lived near one another after the war, we would have stayed the best of friends.

—〰—

I was lucky to survive the war. Once, American soldiers were bombarding the North Koreans and didn't know that some of us were right next to the target. I was sure it was the end for me. Remarkably, no one was injured.

But the most incredible close call I had in Korea happened while I was driving on a country road at early dawn when it was still dark. I'd been told to get to our destination by going over a bridge that crossed a river. I had to keep my headlights off to avoid being spotted, so I couldn't see well. I assumed the bridge was straight ahead and had absolutely no clue that the road to the bridge branched off sharply to the right.

If I had continued going straight, as I'd intended, the road would have suddenly dead-ended at a rushing river and I would have driven right into it. But just as I was about to make that fatal mistake, I suddenly felt something—or someone—grab the wheel and forcefully turn it to the right. A moment later, I drove safely over the bridge.

Although I could never prove it, I was convinced that some force other than my own turned that wheel. It made me wonder if somehow I was meant to survive.

CHAPTER 12: TEAMING UP

WITH SIMON

"I had confidence in one arena: I knew I could always figure
out how to make things work faster and better."

In the summer of 1952, after eight months in Korea, I returned
to America and was transferred to the army reserve. I was twen-
ty-seven and had no direction, no particular skills, and nothing
to do. Simon had an elderly distant cousin who was in the jewelry
manufacturing business, and he talked this man into letting me go
over to his shop to putter around, play with the soldering torch,
and learn a few things. This man taught me how to make settings
for different types and sizes of stones, and then how to turn them
into rings. I worked for him without getting paid so I could break
into the business.

Eventually, I got a job at one of the only two places in the
United States that manufactured a very popular type of wedding
and engagement ring. Tremendous quantities of these rings were

being fabricated and the process required a lot of skilled hand labor. After making the rings for a little while, I came up with an idea for a much more efficient way to produce them.

I imagined a funnel-shaped tool that would grind each ring into a particular shape, leaving room for the setting and stone. It would hold everything together automatically, so all that would need to be done by hand was a little soldering. The process would be fast and require very little labor, and the angles would always be perfect.

It had never occurred to either of the ring companies that there was a way this could be mechanized.

It just so happened that Simon had trained to be a tool and die maker back in Vienna and was extremely skilled and precise at his trade. He was the only person I'd ever heard of with this profession who came from an Orthodox Jewish family—and he was a great thinker, too. I told him, "Listen, I am doing this by hand and every ring has a different shape. If you could make me a tool, I'd have a very simple way of making any size ring very quickly, and then I could really go into business."

Simon made me a great tool, and the owner of the company I worked for let me start my operation there. I told the two ring manufacturers that I would charge them less than it cost them to finish the rings themselves. Because of the savings, and because it was hard to find people who could make a good setting, both companies agreed. They gave me their rings and settings, and I gave them back the finished product.

Part of the process of making the rings included grinding out some of the gold to make room for the settings, so there were gold filings piling up. Not only did I get paid to make the rings, the companies also let me keep the valuable gold filings, which I melted down and resold. As a result, my business became profitable very quickly.

Anybody who could use a torch could immediately make these rings, and before I knew it, I had a few people working for me. I kept my contraption a secret to prevent it from being copied. Soon almost everything was on autopilot and I really didn't have much to do. I was beginning to make money, and I wanted to make even more, so I looked around for other ideas.

Charm bracelets were very popular back then, and the entire industry used clasps that were made by casting pure metals. This was a time-consuming process, and many different sizes were needed to fit the wide variety of bracelet styles and sizes being produced.

I conceived of a way to make clasps for a fraction of the cost by mechanically stamping them out of sheets of metal. I imagined how to manufacture three different sizes that could be cut to any width to fit every bracelet. Also, because I would be stamping out my clasps rather than casting them, I could produce gold-filled snaps that would look like gold on the outside but consist mostly of inexpensive brass. In fact, each clasp would be only 5 percent gold, which would result in a much less expensive product.

Simon and I worked together to figure out how to manufacture this new type of clasp. Without him, I could have never taken the first step. In 1954, we formed Do-All Jewelry, a business in which we were equal partners.

Simon's brother told him he was crazy to leave his steady employment to join forces with me, a "stupid little kid," but Simon didn't listen. Simon had worked for other people for many years and it hadn't gotten him where he wanted to be, so he was willing to take a chance. We started "the shop" in Simon's basement. His brother was afraid we would burn down the house.

Simon and I were the perfect pair. On our own, neither of us was perfect—I could be passive, and sometimes Simon had a temper—but we balanced each other out. We both had patience and respect for one another and never had disagreements.

I didn't like sales and Simon was a natural salesman—gregarious, persuasive, and unafraid of being assertive. He was also skilled and savvy enough to handle the drawings and legal work necessary to get our clasps and manufacturing process patented.

Because our clasps were significantly less costly than clasps made by casting, soon the whole industry was using them. In many ways, Simon and I revolutionized our industry. With seven patents to protect our innovations, we had the competitive advantage for a very long time. When a company in Canada copied our design, they were forced to stop production.

In addition to the gold-filled clasps, Simon and I manufactured gold and silver clasps and continued to innovate new models. Years later, we started producing silver charm bracelets, as well as gold bangle bracelets with beautiful etchings. We formed two new companies to manufacture these products—one named Saviv, which means "circular" in Hebrew, and the other named Rugel, a combination of our two last names, Rubin and Geldwerth.

Once we felt established enough, we rented a space in Manhattan. Later, we moved our operation back to Brooklyn, to a place on 16th Avenue in Borough Park. When we could afford it, we bought a building on 39th Street in Brooklyn. It was approximately 10,000 square feet and we employed three dozen people.

The American dream was coming true for us. Energized by our success, Simon and I were always strategizing new ideas with great enthusiasm for hours on end. Every day, we had lunch at a restaurant called Famous, where we ordered the halibut and talked about our business. We never ran out of things to discuss, and no matter the challenge, together we always managed to come up with the best solution.

Our business excited me, and for a while it gave my life a purpose. It was a relief to finally be successful. As impossible as it had seemed when I was an unhappy, frustrated little boy in Jaworzno, in my daydreams I'd always believed I would be rich when I grew up. I'd actually expected it, and I'd never given up because I had confidence in one arena: I could always figure out how to make things work faster and better.

Once, when I was a boy and Simon was visiting us in Poland, my father had told him, "I think Mendek might make something of himself one day." I was glad that in this instance, my father was right about me.

Because I had been poor for so long, I didn't immediately feel comfortable spending money. I continued to get my hair cut by the barbers in subway stations for $2.00 and bought day-old bagels for half price instead of freshly baked ones.

I never wanted to raise myself above my workers, and Simon and I did our best to compensate them generously. On vacations, I avoided getting tan so it wouldn't be obvious that I had been lounging in the sun while our employees had been hard at work. I continued to sweep the floor of the factory every day. It was a job I enjoyed, and I liked to keep busy. It made me feel good that whenever anything needed fixing in the shop, someone would holler, "Mendek!" and I could usually solve the problem.

Since I was single, Simon brought me back to his house for dinner almost every evening after work. His wife, Cesia, was one of the kindest, most openhearted people I've ever known. She was also a Holocaust survivor, and Bronia and I had befriended her while we were living in Munich after the war. She'd written letters to Simon in America on our behalf. Simon had met her because of us, so we considered ourselves successful matchmakers.

Simon and Cesia had two young daughters, Mizi and Mati. They called me "uncle" and loved to play with my hair. I sang them silly songs I'd picked up, like "Toot, Toot, Tootsie, Good-bye!" I was the only one in the family who owned a car, so I'd often take the girls, along with one or both of their parents, on Sunday outings. We'd spend the day at Prospect Park, where there was a zoo and a merry-go-round, or at Coney Island, where we enjoyed the kiddie rides on the boardwalk. The time

I spent with Mizi and Mati always brought a smile to my lips and lightened my spirits.

I loved Simon like a brother, and because of him and his family, my days were full. But every night, when I returned home to a bare apartment furnished with only a mattress, refrigerator, and television, I was still a bachelor in my late thirties—alone and lonesome.

CHAPTER 13: FINDING EDITH

"We both recognized right away that we belonged to one
another. I never asked her to marry me. We just knew."

I came to the United States with great expectations, and while
I learned to love and appreciate this country, my life lacked
meaning and contentment. Outwardly, no one noticed, but inside
I was in turmoil. In my twenties and thirties, I thought success
and affluence would make me happy. It helped temporarily, but
eventually I reverted to my old, uncomfortable self.

Always weighing on me was my inability to relate to the
opposite sex. Over the years, I'd gone on a handful of dates, but
I'd never met anyone with whom I felt a real connection. One
by one, all my friends from the neighborhood found wives and
started families. Bronia married another Holocaust survivor,
Froim Brandman. They both belonged to a Zionist organization
and met at one of their picnics. They quickly had two daughters,
Etta and Sheindi. Only I remained single.

Although I enjoyed the time I spent with Bronia and Simon's
families, over time I began to feel even more alone. My unhappy
state was something I took for granted, never questioning it or

suspecting that something was amiss. But after fifteen long years in America, I was beginning to think I might not be able to endure my loneliness much longer.

Then one day, in 1961, when I was walking down the street in Borough Park, I ran into my friend Dezsö. He was the only Hungarian friend I had. The rest of the guys were from Poland.

"A group of us are going to Israel on vacation," Dezsö said. "Do you want to join us?"

I'd never been, so I said, "Sure. I'll go."

My friend told me he knew of a single girl in Israel named Edith and asked if I wanted to be introduced.

—m—

Edith was from Hungary, and her father's name was Dezsö, just like my friend. Dezsö wasn't an ordinary Hungarian name. In fact, Edith had never met anyone else with her father's name. So when she heard it was a man named Dezsö who was organizing the meeting between us, she had a good feeling about it.

When Edith and I met, we liked each other right away. Immediately, I wanted to always be near her. It was more than a sexual attraction; it was soul to soul. We both felt it.

Like me, Edith was a Holocaust survivor who had lost every-thing and everyone, except for her sister, Tova. She and Tova had immigrated to Israel in 1948 to be soldiers in the War of Independence. Women weren't allowed in combat and neither of them spoke Hebrew, but because their aptitude tests showed mechanical competence, they had been put to work repairing engines in army vehicles.

When we met, Edith was working at the Israeli Ministry of Education, in charge of managing teacher compensation. She had been unhappily married for seven years and divorced for three.

Edith was a breath of fresh air, very different from all the women I'd met before. It was her frankness that attracted me to her. She expressed her emotions freely and said what was on her mind. During our initial meeting, she told me that she liked me, which I appreciated and thought unusual. The first time we went to the movies, I sat there stiff as a board, dying to hold hands. I believed I wanted her more than she wanted me. It was Edith who reached out and took my hand in hers.

A few nights later, we went for a walk in the park and again held hands as we gazed up at the bright stars. In just a few days, Edith had become the best friend I'd ever had.

Our courtship lasted only nine days. I never asked her to marry me. We both just knew that we belonged to one another. I could have made her my wife then and there, but fear of taking such a huge leap caused me to postpone a union that I knew was inevitable. I flew back to New York, and three months later, Edith was on her way to join me. Air travel was not as common in those days, and Edith was afraid to fly, so I bought her a ticket on the ship *Israel* for a journey that would take two weeks.

Back in Brooklyn, Bronia was shocked by my big news. "How can you do such a thing?" she questioned, "You don't get married after only seeing a person a few times at night. You hardly know her."

Edith had no idea that I was affluent and was sure that she was marrying a man of modest means. In Israel, when she'd asked me what line of work I was in, I'd told her I had a jewelry shop, but I hadn't thought to explain that "the shop" was what we called our busy factory.

Edith had confessed that she wasn't much of a cook. I told her that it didn't matter, as long as she was able to make *lokshen*, which means "noodles" in Yiddish. She said she could do that.

—∽∾∾—

Edith's ship arrived in New York Harbor on the morning of October 30, 1961. I stood at the pier waiting until she cleared customs, both eager and nervous to see her. When our eyes finally met, both of us were scared to death. Our first reaction was disbelief. We felt like total strangers and wondered if we hadn't been too hasty after all. In many ways, we were barely acquainted. I looked at her and thought: *This is for a lifetime. How can I make such a commitment?*

In Israel, we had only seen each other in the daylight once. During the day, both of us had been busy—Edith worked while I went sightseeing. When I visited her in the evenings, we usually spent our time talking in the dark on her front porch.

Now, looking across the water, it was a shock to see each other in full light. But a little while later, when she was in my arms, we shared an unforgettable kiss that reawakened our powerful feelings for each other. Every worry disappeared. I felt like I'd finally come home.

After we drove for a while, I stopped my car to give her a diamond engagement ring. I'd bought a ring of average size and was relieved that it fit perfectly. As we continued on to my apartment, I was pulled over by the police for driving too fast. It was my first ticket ever, but my elation could not be dampened.

Because the holiday *Sukkot* was about to start, Edith and I were married the very next day. Otherwise, we would have had to wait more than a week. Simon arranged the wedding, paid for everything, and was master of ceremonies. I was thirty-seven, Edith, thirty-three.

Our first daughter, Ruthie, was born within a year, and our second daughter, Myra, followed thirteen months later.

CHAPTER 14: THE PRISON

WITHIN ME

"The 'good life' felt like a faraway shore I was always aiming for but could never reach."

Once we were no longer newlyweds, Edith began to watch me with dismay. She could see that my life needed mending even though I wasn't able to acknowledge that something was amiss. The fact that I was frequently sad or depressed didn't catch my attention because I was so used to feeling that way. It was my ordinary existence and I didn't believe it would ever change. While I never questioned my ability to solve a mechanical challenge, when it came to my inner self, I was stuck in helpless inertia.

On the outside, my life was as wonderful as I'd ever hoped it could be. Edith and I bought a new house in a nice neighborhood, full of families with children the same age as ours. Our daughters quickly made good friends, as did we.

Our house had a large backyard where I installed a slide, a swing set, and other play equipment. Our yard quickly became popular with the neighborhood kids. Although neither Edith nor

I had ever heard of celebrating birthdays before leaving Eastern Europe, we threw big parties for our girls each year, like we knew most other families in America did.

I'd never had a pet and didn't know of anyone in my hometown that had owned one, but Edith had grown up with them and wanted a dog for both company and protection. We found a German shepherd that the girls named Star. Over time, I got used to having an animal around to play with and love.

Edith took up oil painting and soon was painting day and night. I'd always been curious about seeing other parts of the world, so we took regular vacations and frequently visited Edith's family in Israel.

Edith became a United States citizen in March of 1966; I'd become one in March of 1953. We were both very grateful to this country, but no matter how secure and pleasant my life appeared, I was still fundamentally unhappy. It wasn't that I was always upset or could never have a good time. Rather, I carried a nagging feeling of emptiness, as if a dark cloud constantly hovered over me.

Having achieved success in both my business and my personal life, I couldn't hope for better circumstances. I was getting on in years and didn't know what else I could do. The "good life" felt like a faraway shore I was always aiming for but could never reach.

My pain was deep, but my thinking was shallow. Avoidance and repression had become my second nature. It felt as if I was living in a house where I only had access to the top floor—a floor with only a few tiny windows that barely allowed a small amount of light and joy to shine in. The lower floors were completely off limits to me. I wasn't sure exactly what went on down there, but I sensed it was the place where all of my fears originated, and I feared my fears more than anything else.

I saw my life, and the lives of the people around me, unfolding along the very same road, leading us nowhere. Over and over, I saw the same horror stories in the newspapers and worried about the same trivialities. Was life really just about so much repetition?

I was gripped with fear about the futility of human existence and plagued by bouts of indifference and resignation.

Just as my physical body had once been imprisoned behind barbed wire barricades, my emotional body was imprisoned behind the barbed wire fences of my psychological makeup. Being poor and hungry hurts, but *feeling* poor hurts just as much. Inner poverty is devastating.

Celebrities like Marilyn Monroe, Judy Garland, and Elvis Presley—to name just a few—are a testimony to inner poverty, a concentration camp of the mind. We all know of people who choose to die because unbearable inner pain makes their lives a living hell. Yet we never hear of people killing themselves because they are hungry.

Suffering of a psychological nature is often harder to bear than physical pain or deprivation. I have suffered both, and the former was much more difficult. When I was hungry, I knew I could quiet my hunger as soon as food became available. But my psychological hunger could not be appeased.

As a child, I had believed that hell was a place one was sent to after death as a punishment for the sins they had committed on earth. But now I realized that hell was not a place outside of me. Hell was the perception that I was alone, separate from the source of life and light that created us all. Hell was right where I was standing.

CHAPTER 15: SEARCHING

FOR ANSWERS

"I had always been curious about how things work, and what was a more challenging puzzle than existence itself?"

L ife in America was very different from life in Israel, but Edith adjusted quickly. Before moving here, my wife had never seen a television, and she was enthralled by the luxury of relaxing at home while being entertained like she was at the theater. Edith had never ridden on a subway, but the day after our wedding she figured out how to take the subway to city hall to pay my speeding ticket. My wife had never had any therapy in Israel, but she knew she needed help, and she was determined to find it. Soon she was taking the subway all over town to participate in encounter groups.

Edith learned about encounter groups from my sister. Very popular in New York City in the mid-1960s, they were a form of self-help group therapy where people got together, often informally, to share and resolve their emotional problems. The groups focused on voicing your feelings publicly, and then receiving feedback and support from other attendees.

Bronia was taking courses in psychology in college, and she and a friend attended many encounter groups together. They even led a few. Bronia recommended a group to Edith that was being run by nuns. My wife decided to go and was immediately hooked. She enjoyed the open atmosphere of these gatherings, where people freely discussed their problems and anxieties.

Like me, Edith suffered from depression. Although hers was more intermittent than mine, she was eager to find relief. She'd had a hard life even before Hitler came to power. Much of her anguish traced back to her early childhood and to her mother, who had been very cruel to her.

Edith and I had much in common. The biggest difference between us was that for a long time I didn't believe I needed help. I was proud, stubborn, and perhaps self-destructive. Nonetheless, Edith was determined to shake me out of my lethargy.

Edith had given birth to Myra while under hypnosis. She said the pain was manageable without medication and she'd felt relaxed the whole time. I found that intriguing, and Edith used my curiosity as an opening. She pointed out the benefits I'd derive from seeing a hypnotherapist and insisted there was nothing to lose. Reluctantly, I agreed.

Edith sent me to someone in Bensonhurst, Brooklyn. To my surprise, I liked both the attention and the novelty it provided. It was relaxing to hear the hypnotherapist's strong, monotone voice communicating soothing words of reassurance: "Now you are relaxed, deeply relaxed, and you are going deeper and deeper . . ."

During that first session, I felt self-assured and happy. It was good to listen to positive, soothing words instead of the negative thoughts that were constantly spinning around in my head. I came home feeling grateful to Edith for her efforts and encouragement. I realized how foolish I'd been to not seek help sooner.

After several hours, however, the euphoria was gone. It had

disappeared into thin air, wiped out by old habits and a mindset that would not give way to anything new.

I saw the hypnotherapist a few more times without noticeable improvement, and then stopped the visits altogether. Nevertheless, it was an important first step. Once my initial resistance had been broken, I was more willing—even eager—to explore new avenues for healing.

Freudian therapy was next on my list. Again, Edith found me a therapist. Psychoanalysis never appealed to me, but I forced myself to go, mostly to please Edith.

That experience was also short-lived. I lay on the couch perplexed, having little to say. I didn't know what was expected of me. Like my father, the therapist was a man of few words. I found his long silences unpleasant and irritating. I didn't understand the benefits of free association and I couldn't get over the hurdle of expressing myself in words as I became aware of my thoughts and feelings.

I walked out of the analyst's office that first day feeling exhausted and disoriented. After my second visit, I lost all desire to go back, but I persisted for four or five more sessions before finally giving up on it.

That was the end of my experimentation with traditional therapy. Edith was disappointed. She couldn't understand why other people went to therapy for years and never ran out of problems to discuss. Why was I so different?

It was around this same time that I became fascinated with theories of psychology. I wanted to learn as much as I could about the human mind, to discover what makes people tick. I had always been curious about how things work, and what was a more challenging puzzle than existence itself? I wanted to figure out the riddle of life, as if I were solving a production challenge in my factory.

Suddenly, overcoming my problems felt like a terribly urgent matter. Even though for decades I'd done nothing about them, I was now very impatient to find a way out of the emotional mess I

was in. I had no idea that I was just beginning the biggest undertaking of my life—one that would require decades of hard work.

—ɯ—

For the next three years, I went "window shopping" for a magic
formula. When I stumbled, I tried again, with Rational therapy,
Gestalt therapy, Feldenkrais therapy, Primal Scream, and other
therapies that were popular during that time.

I was drawn to encounter groups like a magnet. They provided me with an alternative to the inhibitions that prevailed
in society. In these groups, the unspoken and the hidden were
brought out into the open, serving as a relief valve for my unex-
pressed, bottled-up emotions. Listening to people talk freely
about their problems helped me realize I wasn't alone and broke
down my defenses and inhibitions.

I was surprised by the vast array of dissatisfaction and suffering that existed in the world. The conversations in these groups
were less superficial than anything I had encountered thus far,
and they made me see how deep I'd need to go to uncover my
repressed emotions and fears. But as time passed, I began to
realize that these encounter groups weren't resulting in lasting
progress for me or other participants. Eventually, boredom and
stagnation made me lose interest once again.

My search for a method to help me heal continued until
1970, when Edith and I found the Pathwork. The Pathwork was
the beginning of a whole new life for our family.

CHAPTER 16: THE PATHWORK

"It was an oasis of freedom amidst the structure and control of the conventional world."

The Pathwork, often referred to as "the Path," started as a small group, but quickly grew to have a few hundred members. People from all walks of life came together to learn the teachings of an "enlightened spirit" known as the Guide, who was channeled by a charismatic, Austrian-born woman named Eva Pierrakos.

In addition to being the medium for the Guide's esoteric teachings, Eva was the leader of the organization. Her husband, John, a psychiatrist who'd emigrated from Greece before the start of the war, had created a practice called Core Energetics, which focused on unblocking the energies in our bodies associated with negative experiences and emotions. The teachings of the Guide, along with the principles of Core Energetics, were the basis of the "work" we did in the Pathwork.

Edith and I were early members. To be in the presence of the Guide, we traveled into Manhattan every week for an evening gathering at a member's apartment in SoHo. With candles and incense burning on an altar in front of her, we all watched in awe as Eva went into a trance and made room within her for another being to enter. Her body would suddenly fall forward and then right itself. Sitting up very straight, she'd take several loud, quick breaths in through her nose, and then the Guide would begin to speak through her in an accent notably different from her own.

Looking back, I can't say whether it was real or not. As far-fetched as it may sound now, it felt authentic to me at the time.

The Guide alternated between giving a lecture one week and a question and answer session the next. The talks touched on topics such as, "Self-Will, Pride, and Fear," "The Higher Self, The Lower Self, and the Mask," "Compulsion to Recreate and Overcome Childhood Hurts," and "The Life Force in the Universe." These lectures were transcribed for Pathwork members to read and study. I found the wisdom to be very inspiring.

A cornerstone of the Pathwork was the idea that we must "work on ourselves" to transform our conscious and unconscious negativity, which we called our "Lower Self," into positive energy. As our Lower Self was revealed and eliminated, we'd have more space for our "Higher Self" to emerge. The Guide explained that reincarnation was part of the human development process, and that we'd keep being reborn until we achieved an elevated state of consciousness, which meant living from our Higher Self, not our egos.

In the early years, Eva or John met with every Pathwork member individually to help us progress. As the organization grew and this became impossible, they formed a "Training Group" to teach senior members to serve as "helpers" for newer members. For those of us who'd been having sessions with Eva for years, no previous experience was required.

Edith and I became helpers and began to give weekly sessions to many people, using the principles and techniques of the Pathwork to help them resolve a wide variety of issues. We also worked together as co-helpers, giving sessions to couples wanting to use Pathwork methods to improve their relationships.

As the Pathwork continued to grow, additional training groups were formed, and our group became known as "Training Group One." With the formation of every new group, our status as members of the first training group grew.

In addition to private sessions, everyone in the Pathwork had to attend groups that utilized Gestalt and encounter group principles. Eva or John led some of these groups, and high-level members led others. People took turns sitting in the center of the circle to work on themselves as others looked on and gave feedback. Most members had dramatic breakthroughs. It wasn't uncommon for people to cry as if their hearts were breaking while the rest of us reassured them by saying, "It's okay. We love you." Such cathartic experiences were exciting and inspiring.

The biggest group was the weekly "Saturday Night Group" at the Center. There was also a special "Couples Group" for people in committed relationships, and if anyone was in crisis, he or she could initiate a group to focus on their specific issue. Even the children of adult members had to attend either the "Children's Group" or the "Teenage Group," and they had helpers they met with weekly as well.

Our fellow Pathwork members included carpenters, farmers, university professors, physicians, famous individuals, as well as people on welfare. Social standing was irrelevant. We believed that our basic humanity ran deeper than our differences. The motivation that brought us together was varied, but one common denominator was that all of us felt something was lacking in our lives and believed the Pathwork would fill that need.

Overall, the principles of the Pathwork seemed sound, and I was impressed by the progress we made. The Pathwork gave me much-needed hope and a reason for living. It wiped away my depression and dispelled my sense of alienation and loneliness. I had found a new way of life that suited my temperament and made me feel fulfilled. I belonged, I believed, and I was having fun. High on my newfound good luck, I was confident that all my troubles would soon be over.

—⚮—

The Pathwork grew quickly in spite of the fact that the obligatory sessions and groups were expensive. Some members spent a large part of their income on these activities. Any perceived slackening of commitment to the Pathwork was considered the work of the Lower Self.

Coupled with the desire for self-improvement was a prevailing sense of mission. We believed that we were the carriers of original knowledge that the world at large was in need of, even if the world didn't know it yet. I felt as if I was among a select group of "chosen people" all over again.

Edith and I became two of the Pathwork's most active and enthusiastic members, and we were among its biggest financial supporters. In 1972, we helped fund the acquisition of a former resort on a beautiful piece of property in the countryside of upstate New York, in a small town named Phoenicia. The group named it the Center for the Living Force, but we referred to it as "the Center."

Our family began to spend every weekend and all summer at the Center. Ruthie and Myra slept on bunk beds in the girls' dorm, while Edith and I had a private room in a motel-style building at the far end of the property. We all ate our meals communally in the dining hall, once in a while as a family, but most often with our peers. There were many children around the same age as our daughters, and they were all the best of friends.

What excited me the most about the Center was the feeling of adventure we all felt there. It was an oasis of freedom amidst the structure and control of the conventional world. I made friends with like-minded individuals, people who also considered themselves rebels. For the first time, I thought I was a free man. I could allow myself to be who I was, without fear or censorship.

At the Center, we enjoyed fresh air and fresh-picked vegetables from a garden. There was a lovely pond for swimming in the summer and ice-skating in winter. The property had a big barn where we held large workshops and threw dance parties on Saturday nights. The members of a professional rock band were in the Pathwork, and they played for us frequently.

We let our imaginations run wild, and improvised events like the "Egyptian Pageant," where we all dressed up in elaborate costumes and marched in a long procession while playing musical instruments. It culminated in a ceremony we created that made it seem like we'd made a dry creek run with water again.

The freedom I felt to express myself in the Pathwork brought out some innate abilities I had no idea I possessed. I discovered that I loved to write and began jotting down my revelations. Later, I turned them into poems and affirmations to help me access my Higher Self more easily. I carried my writings with me so they'd always be on hand for contemplation and inspiration. Eventually, I shared my writings with other members by creating "Higher Self Cards" that were small enough to fit in a pocket. I asked a gifted artist in the Pathwork to illustrate them, and then printed many sets that I distributed freely.

—ɯ—

As the Pathwork became the center of our family's life, we drifted away from the "real world." Because we were at the Center every weekend, we stopped socializing with our neighbors in Brooklyn, and our daughters weren't available for typical friendships with peers. The Pathwork wasn't something we could easily explain to outsiders, so we kept quiet about how we were spending our time. We hardly saw my relatives, except on special occasions like weddings. Simon and Bronia were upset and worried. They feared we'd lost our minds.

CHAPTER 17: DISMANTLING
MY FORTRESS

"When I could no longer put the blame on other people—or even on God—I was free to create my own destiny."

My time in the Pathwork was a crash course in human nature. Getting to know people in the raw was sometimes more than I bargained for, but it was enlightening. Many of the illusions I had about myself and others were shattered in the process.

I realized that many people, myself included, lived as if we were occupying a fortress in need of defending. We desperately wanted love and approval from others, but at the same time we guarded against being vulnerable. Through so much group interaction, I learned that I wasn't the only one subconsciously begging everyone to love me, validate me, and make me feel good about myself. I wasn't the only one silently judging others, seeking out their weaknesses and vulnerabilities. Everyone projected their shortcomings, formed stereotypes, and deluded themselves with false superiority.

Before the Pathwork, I didn't realize that I had adopted a defensive posture against attack and that this had become my second nature. I didn't understand or want to know what I was hiding or defending against, so I relegated it to my subconscious. Trying to protect my secrets from both myself and others, I lived with a constant fear of being discovered.

The nice guy I thought I was—the one who was always so agreeable and pleasing, who liked to keep things low-key and never raise a storm—was not such an accommodating fellow after all. My benevolent, smiling exterior was a mask that hid a cold, petty personality bent on getting his way in life. When other people in the Pathwork weren't fooled and saw through my pretense, I squirmed and wanted to lash out.

Over time, I began to realize that it would be impossible for me to live up to the idealized self-image I'd long felt compelled to present to the world. Thankfully, I began to learn to let it go.

—◆—

In the Pathwork, we believed there are no coincidences, and that we all create our own reality. If someone was out of work, sick, or lonely—even if they were in an accident—it was all their own doing. On some level, they derived negative pleasure from it.

While this philosophy sometimes went overboard, it was actually very empowering for me. As I learned to take full responsibility for everything that happened in my life, I stopped attributing my troubles to forces outside myself. And when I could no longer put the blame on other people—or even on God—I became free to create my own destiny.

Yes, I had been victimized. But that did not mean I had to identify as a victim for the rest of my days. I'd spent decades wallowing in my suffering and wanting the world to feel sorry for me. A stubborn part of me was still clinging to my old ways and was not yet ready or willing to release my anger and bitterness. It would take a superhuman effort to unearth and change these patterns, but I had to do it. The price I was paying for my helplessness wasn't just pain, it was the loss of my free will.

What I came to realize was that the antidote to being a victim was to stop giving credence to the lie that I was a helpless bystander in my life. My old refrain had been, "Never will I trust again." Suffering felt natural to me; happiness did not. I had to let go of these outdated, useless emotional and mental habits if I wanted to construct my life anew.

The Pathwork had methods to help us get rid of the negativity we were storing, but the first step was a willingness to unearth and face it. In both private sessions and in groups, we spent a great deal of time "giving out anger." Often, we used "batakas," thick foam bats covered in red fabric with handles, to hit pillows or mattresses as hard as we could. Simultaneously, we'd yell at the target of our anger, "NO!" or "I HATE YOU!"

The theory was that once our skeletons were out of the closet, our negativity would no longer pose a threat to us or others. We also worked to find the courage to let go of our "Mask Self," the false personality we try to maintain so that others will approve of us.

With our jealousy and contempt out in the open for all to see, it became clear that almost everyone felt superior to someone else. This fascinated me. I was surprised that people I thought little of—those who couldn't hold down a job or form a relationship—felt they were better than me. Most of us walked around like peacocks, silently and secretly finding reasons to be proud of ourselves, even though another part of us felt just the opposite.

In groups, we were commanded to let out our "Negative Intentionality" by expressing all of our irrational emotions, including our venom and judgments about one another. When we saw a person unmask these types of thoughts without inhibition, it became easier for others to break down their resistance as well. The groups often became a source of high drama.

When it was your turn to work, you had to be careful not to appear to complain or whine, because that would only make everyone laugh at you. But if you shared the details of your hidden sadistic desires, proving you were the scum of the earth with no redeeming features whatsoever, you would be warmly applauded for doing your best work.

In one workshop, the leader told a good friend of mine—who was also a Holocaust survivor who'd lost most of his family in the war—to act as if he was a member of the Gestapo. The idea was that instead of being a victim, he'd learn what it was like to be the aggressor.

My friend assumed the role very convincingly. He yelled and screamed at everyone with so much anger and fervor that we all became terrified. Edith was never comfortable being around him after that. Nonetheless, my friend said this exercise led him to discover that he'd been trying to bury all of his aggression since the war, including the aspects of it that he needed to stay motivated and confident. He felt the experience enabled him to begin to reclaim positive parts of his manhood.

—m—

One summer day, as we were prospecting new ways to unearth our Lower Selves, someone came up with an idea about how we could fully excavate our dislike for one another. He called it "The Contempt Group." Many members, including Edith and me, jumped at the opportunity to be a part of this.

We quickly assembled and headed out to the woods that same afternoon. The weather was perfect. We squatted on the ground in a circle and immediately let go on each other. We wanted to unleash our Lower Selves to new heights and had no time to waste. Each of us took our turn standing up to face everybody in the circle. One by one, we each had the opportunity to share every hateful criticism we could think of.

Not surprisingly, instead of helping us, the Contempt Group made us all feel terrible. Edith told a woman who'd been a close friend that she thought she was ugly. Unfortunately, her honesty permanently soured their relationship.

One of the participants was a young man in his early twenties who regularly visited my family at our home in Brooklyn. When it was his turn, he faced me, then proceeded to share his hostility toward the Jewish people, myself included. "My one regret," he said, "was that Hitler didn't finish the job. He should have killed you all." I had no idea such thoughts were in his head until that day. In another situation, I would never have spoken to him again for the rest of my life. In the Pathwork, I had no choice but to learn to live with it.

In contrast, other groups showed me how people can help each other heal. During one Saturday Night Group, a German woman worked on her grief over losing her father during the war when she was two years old. He had been a soldier fighting for Germany on the Russian Front when he was killed.

As the woman was reliving her loss and crying out for her father, I could feel the depth of her pain. I got up and went to embrace her. "I will be your father," I said, and cradled her in my arms and rocked her until the grieving passed and she fell into a deep slumber.

CHAPTER 18: UNEARTHING

MY PAST

"By denying my love, I'd denied myself the pleasures of loving, and I'd paid a great price for my inhibitions."

Weekend intensives took place at the Center several times a year. We'd arrive in the country on Friday evening, divide into groups of about fifteen people, and devote the weekend to work designed to go deep.

Each intensive had a specific focus, and one particular weekend the focus was on our unresolved feelings toward our parents.

Growing up, my fury toward my father was my greatest secret. His silent anger and disapproval loomed heavily in my mind, and I blamed him for all my suffering. I pretended I was unaffected by our difficult relationship and put up a front of cold indifference, but underneath, my hurt and anger were so great that I sometimes wished he were dead. I always lived in fear that he'd discover my true feelings.

I had no idea that completely different emotions were buried underneath my hostility. Deep within me, I had strong, unfulfilled longings for my father's love and affection and desperately wanted his approval. But never in a million years could I have admitted this to myself. I felt so self-conscious about these feelings that even now, part of me prefers to deny them.

Neither of my parents openly expressed affection toward each other or their children, except when we were babies, so I concluded that tender sentiments were stupid and painful, a sign of weakness I had to hide. But I felt no such hesitations about my anger. Anger came naturally to me, and I believed it was a sign of strength. I didn't yet realize that love and hate are related, opposite sides of the same coin. So I was completely unprepared for what unfolded during this intensive.

When my turn came, I suddenly heard myself begin to talk about the Holocaust. I couldn't believe it. It was the first time in my life that I'd ever shared what I knew about Auschwitz, the gas chambers, and the manner in which my parents, and almost everyone I knew from my hometown, had died. I'd never even discussed it with Edith, who had been there.

The Holocaust was too big a wound to tear open. The only way I'd been able to move forward had been to pay as little attention to it as possible. Both Edith and I maintained that our major emotional challenges came from our very difficult relationships with our parents—she with her mother and me with my father— and not from the war.

Now, despite my resistance, something made me go on and on. I spoke in a matter-of-fact manner, giving a mechanical recital of events, as if I was talking about the weather. But suddenly, I became overwhelmed with grief so intense, I went into shock. I felt a piercing pain in my chest, as if I was being exposed to a high-voltage wire. It was like being ripped apart, and I was sure I was having a heart attack.

I was overtaken with a sadness and despair so acute it felt unbearable. My voice failed me. The pain was physical, mental and emotional. I couldn't tell which hurt more. I didn't know where the suffering was coming from or how it could ever end. My memory went blank. When I tried to talk to the leader, I couldn't remember his name. I couldn't recall the names of the other people in the group, even though I knew them all well.

After perhaps ten or fifteen minutes, the intense pain started to lessen. Slowly, I began to feel exceptionally tender and loving toward both my mother and father, an unbreakable bond of caring and kinship between us that could only be described as other-worldly. I had an intense desire to assist them, as if they were my own children, crying out for help. I felt dismayed and frustrated at my helplessness. They seemed to exist in another dimension of time.

I no longer cared whether my father deserved my respect and affection. What mattered was that I had deprived myself of something essential by repressing my love for him. By hiding behind my defenses and denying my love, I'd denied myself the pleasures of loving, and I'd paid a great price for my inhibitions.

That experience brought me back to profound love and loss. It showed me the pristine purity and freshness that come with love's tenderness and affection. As a child, I had loved because love comes naturally—because love is our reason for living.

I realized that I could love that way again.

CHAPTER 19: A TIME OF GRACE

"The old, fearful part of me stepped aside, making room for something new and wonderful to enter."

Every winter, a group of high-level Pathwork members went skiing together in Arosa, Switzerland. Edith and I never would have gone if we hadn't been strongly encouraged to do so. My background and education had not prepared me for this kind of luxury. Although I'd been affluent for almost two decades, I still felt poor, retaining patterns that kept my vision narrow and my aspirations modest. My mind was used to thinking in terms of scarcity and limitation. I'd never even read a book or seen a movie until I was in my twenties.

As a little boy in Poland, I'd often hidden behind a wooden fence at night during the winter and looked into an ice-skating rink where the gentiles were enjoying their favorite sport. I hadn't even known that I was supposed to be jealous. Skating was against tradition, and so off limits that I dared not tell my parents I was even watching. Were I to live to be a hundred, I could never have pictured myself skiing down the Alps.

Yet those two weeks we spent in Arosa were a blissful inter-lude where I felt an ever-present joy and rapture. It was as if I had stepped into a new, beautiful planet—a world outside of this world. It was a time of grace, when the old, fearful part of me stepped aside, making room for something new and wonderful to enter. I was happy to be alive.

We flew into Zurich, and the next morning boarded a sin-gle-rail train in the small town of Chur, situated at the foot of the Alps. Seeming to defy the force of gravity, the train huffed and puffed its way higher and higher as an exquisite landscape unfolded before my eyes.

Riding in a railroad car that appeared to be suspended in midair simultaneously gave me a sinking stomach and a sense of exhilaration. As we traversed rail bridges that miraculously spanned majestic mountain ridges, my eyes were riveted on the countless pools, rivulets, and little waterfalls hurrying downhill.

The town of Arosa was nestled in a valley that seemed like the womb of the mountains—a haven of peace and tranquility. I was mesmerized.

After we left our luggage in our hotel room, I behaved like a little boy on a day off from school, eager to explore the wonders of creation. I just couldn't wait to get to the top of the mountains, where the action was. As our gondola lifted away from the station, a panoramic scene came into view. The sun was close; the sky, bright blue. The entire heavens poured their light onto the earth below as an endless parade of skiers glided down the snow-cov-ered mountains, seemingly coming out of nowhere.

Sensing this joyous outpouring of movement and grace, I felt that everything was in harmony with the One who created it—a God of pure love and serenity. It was a mystical experience, a religious awakening. I suddenly heard myself reciting a Jewish prayer from my childhood that I'd long ago forgotten.

I never learned to ski well, but I didn't care. Being clumsy on the slopes didn't stop me from experiencing the rapture of playing

like a child. I took T-bars, ski lifts, and gondolas to the moun-
taintops, and every time I skied down, I felt like I was floating
in midair. The freedom was exhilarating. When I wasn't skiing,
I sat by the window in our hotel room for hours, watching huge
snowflakes fall on the town below.

Arosa awakened my spiritual sensitivity to the sublime and
the profound. Never before had I perceived God to be an all-en-
compassing energy of pure love and beauty—not the judgmental,
omnipotent dictator of my childhood. While I was in Arosa, for
the first time in my life, I believed that the world was a kind and
magnificent place.

The hard part was coming down from the mountains. It was
a coming down in spirit as well, an inevitable descent into the "real
world"—a place from which there was no escape.

CHAPTER 20: BREAKING AWAY

"A spell had been broken. My eyes suddenly opened."

For years, our family spent weekdays in Brooklyn eagerly waiting for Friday afternoon, when we could return to the Center. We felt more at home there than in the city. The Center was where we could be with our closest friends and colleagues—people who shared our belief system and spiritual aspirations. It was where we felt the comfort, support, and security of being part of a community.

I loved being in the country and was soothed by the beauty and energy of nature. Edith loved the countryside, too, and enjoyed not having to shop for food or cook. While our inner work in the Pathwork could be challenging, in many ways, we lived like we were on vacation while we were there.

Edith had grown spiritually powerful and had blossomed into a well-respected leader. She ran two popular groups—"Journey to the Higher Self" and "The Psychic Group"—as well as weekend intensives. We were helpers to many people for whom we cared deeply. As the years passed, it seemed only natural to move to the Center full time.

We were the first family to build a private house on the property. When it was finished in 1976, we sold our house in Brooklyn and settled in. Our new home was located on the hillside just beyond the main buildings. Our family continued to eat all our meals in the communal dining room, so we hardly used our new kitchen, but it was nice to have more than the one small bedroom we'd occupied for so long, and to have the girls sleep in our house instead of in the girls' dorm.

The bottom floor was a big open space, thickly carpeted and designed to accommodate Edith's groups, during which people lay in a circle as she led them through the various exercises and visualizations she'd developed. We encircled the room with large, beautiful gemstones believed to have powerful healing energy, including amethysts, quartz, lapis, and topaz. There was also a separate room downstairs where we could hold private sessions.

We enrolled the girls in the local public school—Myra in eighth grade, Ruthie in ninth. I still ran my business with Simon but changed my schedule to work four days a week. I drove into the city early each Monday morning, and returned to the Center late each Thursday night.

We never could have imagined that within a year of moving to the Center, disenchantment with the Pathwork would begin to set in. But after having devoted seven years of my life to this organization, I was beginning to have doubts. The novelty was gone, and unearthing and owning up to my Lower Self had become mechanical and unproductive. Perhaps the Pathwork had outlived its usefulness for me.

As the Pathwork continued to grow, more structure was necessary and there wasn't as much room for experimentation, innovation, or spontaneity. No matter how noble its intent, the Pathwork had become an institution that thrived on conformity and precluded freedom of thought. I was part of a community where people were allowed to swim naked in public, yet I felt confined and restricted. It was no longer a lot of fun. I felt as if a spell had been broken.

At the same time, Edith began questioning Eva's motives and integrity, which put these two strong women in direct conflict. Eva felt threatened by Edith and grew suspicious of her and unkind.

While I shared Edith's concerns, I wasn't as passionate about them as she was. I'd always been less vocal and tried to avoid confrontation. But as Edith grew increasingly disturbed and unhappy, the situation became stressful and uncomfortable for us all.

During the summer of 1977, we decided we wanted out.

Our departure from the Pathwork was excruciatingly painful. As the first high-level members to leave, we encountered a tremendous amount of resistance, anger, and resentment. In the past, whenever someone had disagreed with the leader or had an opinion at odds with the one prevailing in the community, the dissenting opinion had been said to arise from that person's Lower Self. When newer members had doubts or decided to quit, everyone assumed it was because the individual, not the organization, was flawed. But now, two members of the original training group were leaving, and the leaders—who felt deeply threatened—responded by totally discrediting us.

Because Edith was more outspoken, she became Eva's sole target. Eva sent a letter to members stating that Edith had gone astray and everyone should renounce their relationship with her.

High-level members tried all kinds of strategies to get me to stay. I was told that I was being overly influenced by Edith, and I began to doubt my decision to leave. I agreed to go to the Center for an intensive to get in touch with my true feelings before making a final decision. At that point, even my marriage felt threatened.

While I was packing my bag for the weekend intensive, Edith and the girls cried and begged me not to go. I felt confused and tormented, yet determined to follow through. But when Edith said,

"Don't let them play with your mind," I could suddenly see that was exactly what was happening—the leaders were trying to tear us apart. That's when I decided to stop questioning whether or not I should quit. I chose to stay where I belonged—with my family.

—⚏—

Leaving the Pathwork was a huge strain emotionally, especially for Edith. She felt attacked and deeply hurt by the Pathwork members she'd considered her closest friends. If anyone from the organization reached out to her, they were accused of not being loyal to the Pathwork, so few people stayed in touch.

I was afraid that leaving the Pathwork would cause me to relapse into my former state of apathy and depression. I dreaded going back to my loneliness. Quitting was like letting go of my crutches. I was venturing out on my own, leaving behind the group that had been woven into my life for so long. Yet simultaneously, I was tired of my long commutes back and forth to the city. I needed rest and looked forward to going back to a more normal, subdued lifestyle.

Perhaps we should have quit sooner, but I'd been too scared.

I didn't realize how much our abrupt decision to leave the Pathwork would impact our daughters, who had grown up in that community. It broke Myra's heart to have to say good-bye to the children she babysat for, her "helper" of many years, and "The Boutique"—a popular business she'd started where she sold members' used clothes on consignment to other members.

Ruthie had never liked living at the Center full time and desperately wanted to move back to the city. But all her closest friends were part of the Pathwork, and she didn't want to lose them. Unfortunately, Edith took any contact Ruthie had with people in the Pathwork as a personal betrayal and forced her to make a clean break.

When we left the Pathwork, we had to abandon our home at the Center without any financial compensation. We bought a two-bedroom apartment on East 86th street in Manhattan, and during those first months, Edith avoided leaving the apartment altogether because she feared running into someone from the organization.

Thus, we began a new phase of our lives—sad, scared, and shell-shocked.

CHAPTER 21: FINDING MY OWN PATH

"Meditating helped me begin to question the sovereignty of my mind."

A new chapter in my life began after we left the Pathwork. Until then, I'd been seeking outside help and guidance in my spiritual and psychological explorations. Now, at fifty-two, it was time for me to embrace my own independence.

I have no regrets about my participation in the Pathwork. Every experience was part of a spiritual safari that widened my horizons and expanded my outlook. Each step I took was timely and necessary, preparing the ground for what was to come.

Edith and I credit the Pathwork's technique of "giving out anger" with helping to lift our depression. It was cathartic for us to acknowledge our pent-up fury, express it through screaming, kicking, and stomping, and then let it go. "Giving out anger" helped us come to terms with the horrors we'd lived through and make room for more positive emotions. We continued using these methods for years.

It was also in the Pathwork that we began to meditate, and meditation has remained a staple of my spiritual work. Meditating helped me see the true nature of my mind—it was constantly wandering, with fearful and upsetting notions running on without end. The practice gave me a new perspective and helped me begin to question the sovereignty of my mind.

The Pathwork was also where I saw how helpful it was to put my revelations into words. Writing clarified my ideas and reinforced my discoveries. After we left the Pathwork, I wrote more than ever. I always carried a pen and paper in one of my pockets so I could jot down ideas as soon as they came to me.

Before the Pathwork, Edith had encouraged me to try my hand at painting. Once we left and I finally had the time, I began to paint frequently, with great enthusiasm. The designs and figures that surfaced from my subconscious always surprised and intrigued me.

Not long after our move to Manhattan, we started missing the countryside, so we bought a small vacation home in Southampton, a few miles from the ocean. Our whole family spent time there during the warmer months, but I was the only one who was drawn there regularly in winter. I often went alone on the weekends and walked the beach every day, no matter the temperature. I loved how empty it was. It was those Southampton walks that inspired me to take up photography.

Both Edith and I continued exploring a wide variety of spiritual teachings. She was drawn to the Hindu philosophy of Swami Sivananda, which led her to discover an oceanfront Sivananda yoga retreat in the Bahamas. To vacation there, you had to adhere to their rigorous practice schedule, which included long morning and evening meditation and chanting sessions, as well as twice-daily yoga classes. Our family went there many times. Those trips provided the relaxation and solace we all needed.

In 1980, both our girls went away to college. That time—just the two of us, without our daughters—was an era of deep healing, especially for Edith. She was still recovering from the trauma of leaving the Pathwork, as well as her sister's untimely death at the age of forty-seven. Edith and I began spending more time in Southampton. We took long walks on the beach every day and often gave out anger together, stomping our way through the soft sand.

Every night, we went to our favorite restaurant, built over the water on the bay. In addition to the delicious food, we enjoyed the view, watching the river otters play, and had wonderful conversations. We had no idea how dramatically our life was about to change.

CHAPTER 22: CALIFORNIA

"When I looked at the ocean, I knew I wanted to always be near it. The time had come to relocate to a place with so much beauty."

After her freshman year in Boston, our older daughter, Ruthie, transferred to the University of California in Santa Cruz. In 1982, Edith and I visited her there. We'd never been to Northern California and were eager to explore the area, so the three of us took a weekend trip to the nearby Monterey Peninsula. While Edith was resting at the hotel, Ruthie and I took a drive around 17 Mile Drive in Pebble Beach.

The landscape and coastline were mesmerizing. When I looked at the ocean, I knew I wanted to always be near it. The time had come to relocate to a place with so much beauty.

Back at the hotel, I told Edith I had fallen in love with California and was ready to move. She immediately agreed. Just like when we met and decided to get married so quickly—and like every other major decision in our lives—we both just knew these things and never disagreed.

Three days later, we bought a house in Carmel.

After almost thirty years, I was ready to retire. For decades, Simon and I had worked day and night, as if our lives depended on it. Our business wasn't easy. It was one headache after another. We'd always persevered, but I was getting fed up. I was tired of leaving for work at 6:00 a.m. every morning, and sick of having to worry about robberies—a constant concern because of the large amounts of gold and silver we had to keep on hand.

My interests had shifted from business to the spiritual realm. I wanted the freedom to go where I wanted to go and do what I wanted to do, and I had enough money to do that. So, when someone came along who wanted to buy our business, Simon and I both agreed to the sale. Just like that, a very significant era of my life came to a close.

I was not quite sixty and I was officially retired. My time was my own!

Edith had grown up on a farm in Hungary and had always wanted the opportunity to experience that lifestyle again. She loved nature, animals, and eating fruit right from the tree. So, after living in Carmel for a year, we bought a two-and-a-half-acre raspberry farm in Carmel Valley, adjacent to the Carmel River, less than a fifteen-minute drive from our house. It needed work, but the raspberries were delicious, and the property had over one hundred fruit and nut trees.

During this time, Myra was trying to figure out what she wanted to do between college and graduate school, so she and her boyfriend, Drew, moved onto the farm. It was the summer of 1984, and Edith and I let them live there for free in exchange for helping with the improvements. Drew was also from New York, and both he and Myra were eager to live in the country, work with their hands, and learn to farm.

Drew and Myra started harvesting the raspberries right away. They sold them at a roadside stand and also delivered them to local restaurants and markets. Soon, they named their little operation Earthbound Farm.

In the beginning, we all worked together. I helped Myra and Drew remove all the old wooden stakes and wires supporting the raspberry bushes and build new trellises. It was enjoyable to teach my daughter how to measure and cut posts, the best way to hammer nails into wood, and how to drill perfectly perpendicular holes.

Building things gave me pleasure, so I constructed a storage shed with windows that had different shapes and painted the window trim sky blue. Then I added on a shelter for the tractor. I never worked from a plan, because figuring out designs in my head was a fun challenge. It was wonderful having so many projects. I took excursions to the lumberyard to select the wood I needed and welcomed the tricky task of fitting the long boards into my car.

But what I loved most were my trips to the hardware store. Growing up, my family's hardware store had always felt like a toy store to me, and the ones in California were huge. They had everything I needed, and many things I never knew existed. Once inside, I never wanted to leave.

Myra and Drew farmed organically, without any chemicals, so they used a lot of compost. I invented a system with six different mixers to make compost out of weeds and waste quickly, in a small amount of space. I also built a contraption to sift the finished product. To pick raspberries, I devised a handy container that attached to your waistband or belt to free up both your hands. It rocked as you moved, so it always stayed upright and never spilled. Edith and I often pitched in when the berries needed to be harvested, as did everyone else who visited.

Drew and Myra had two big dogs, Zephyr and Flick, who followed me around as I worked. They were good company, and also great examples of how to live. They didn't fret about tomorrow or regret what happened yesterday. Instead, they took pleasure where they could find it and gave affection unconditionally.

—∭—

Myra and Drew fell in love with farm living and began growing new crops in addition to raspberries—herbs, baby lettuces, and specialty salad greens. In the fall of 1986, soon after they got married, they decided they wanted to try and sell their organic baby greens already washed and packaged in plastic bags. No one had ever done this before.

At the time, they were washing the salad in their kitchen sink, then packing and labeling each bag by hand, one by one. This was very time-consuming. Fortunately, figuring out how to mechanize their operation was right up my alley. My greatest talent in business had always been organizing things to produce a top-quality product quickly, and with the least amount of labor.

It took a lot of experimentation to figure out the best way to pack the salad. I got most of the parts I needed from a huge junkyard a half hour away. It was like a big treasure hunt every time I went there. I found the things I needed to make a packing line for almost no money. As Drew and Myra's business got bigger, they hired employees and we moved the packing lines I'd designed from their deck into their living room, which became a small salad-packing factory.

Drew and Myra had a shed built next to their house for washing the salad and commissioned the three extra-large custom-made metal sinks we needed for the triple-washed lettuce system I'd devised. Using an arrangement of pulleys attached to the shed's ceiling, the lettuce was moved from one sink to another, into cleaner and clearer water as the dirt was washed away. Eventually, I also invented an automatic "dunker" to gently agitate the salad during each of the washes, so it didn't have to be done by hand. This was tricky, because baby greens are delicate. It was a big challenge to get them clean without crushing them.

After the washing system was working well, I tried to create a filter system that would thoroughly clean the dirty water so it could be reused. This was never entirely successful, but I enjoyed the challenge nonetheless.

—ɯɯ—

After a few years, Drew and Myra's business became so successful that they no longer needed my help. But after spending so much time on the farm, Edith and I had grown to prefer the sunny weather in Carmel Valley to the climate in Carmel, where it was often foggy and cold during the summer. In 1989, we bought a house in Carmel Valley on top of a hill, less than a mile from the farm.

It was the first time Edith and I had ever lived in a home that had breathtaking views. The sunsets were exquisite, and I loved to photograph the brilliant shades of red that covered the sky. Our backyard had a small lawn bordered by a rocky hillside, which I transformed into a beautiful rock garden with Buddhas, a fountain, and many large pieces of semi-precious stones. I turned the garage into my workshop and bought every tool that caught my eye. Even if I didn't have a use for it just yet, I knew eventually it would come in handy. I still had inventions forming in my mind that I wanted to play around with.

I drove to the beach for my walks almost every day, and I began to write in earnest. Edith and I took regular excursions to discover more of the natural splendor of our local area. In California, we were surrounded by beauty everywhere we looked, and we never took it for granted.

*Mendek's family in Poland. Front row, left to right: Mendek,
sister Bronia, cousin Liba, sister Rutka, brother Tuleg.
Back Row, left to right: mother Ida, sister Mila, father Israel.*

*Mendek's family in Poland. Front row, left to right: Mendek,
sister Mila, sister Macia, cousin Simon, cousin Liba, father Israel.
Back Row, left to right: brother tuleg, sister Rutka, sister Bronia.*

Mendek's father, Israel

Mendek's sisters Mila, Bronia,
and Rutka in Jaworzno, 1936

Mila on the streets
of Jaworzno, Winter 1937

Mendek's family home in Jaworzno

Mendek in his twenties

*Mendek with Simon and Bronia
in America, 1946*

Mendek and Yu in Korea, circa 1952

*Bronia's wedding day, 1953. Left to right: Mendel Geldwerth
(Simon's brother), Regi (Mendel's wife), Mendek, Bronia, Tzirel
(Simon's mother), Cesia (Simon's wife), Mizi (Simon's daughter)
and Simon. Boys in front: Avi and Lipa (Mendel and Regi's sons).*

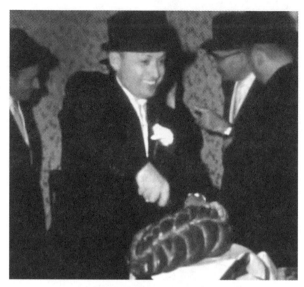

Mendek and Edith's wedding reception,
October 31, 1961

Mendek and Edith's wedding reception,
October 31, 1961

Edith, Ruthie, Mendek,
and Myra, circa 1965

*Mendek and Simon in their jewelry factory
in Brooklyn, mid-1970s*

Mendek in the Pathwork, late 1970s

*Mendek and Edith at their first house
in Carmel, CA, 1982*

Mendek and Myra building raspberry supports, 1984

Mendek and Drew experimenting with
lettuce washing methods, 1986

Mendek and Ruthie on Earthbound Farm's new tractor, late 1980s

Myra with Marea, Mendek,
newborn Jeffrey, and Drew, 1992

Mendek and Jeffrey on the farm, 1995

Mendek and Marea, 1996

A sampling of Mendek's booklets, jewelry, and art

Mendek and Edith with granddaughter Nina, 2002

Mendek and Myra singing their favorite Hebrew songs, 2009

Mendek and Edith on Edith's birthday, 2009

PART III:

The World Inside Me

CHAPTER 23:

THE MECHANICAL MIND

"I was trapped by my beliefs like an animal in a cage."

Ever since I was a young man, I'd sensed that human beings were creatures of arbitrary habits. At the end of the war, when I looked into the eyes of a German soldier my age, I'd been surprised to recognize our common humanity. More than our uniforms and ethnicity, what separated us was our conditioning. If the two of us had been raised by the other's parents in the other's hometown, it's likely I would have been the soldier carrying the gun and he the starving, brutalized inmate.

But as I got older and increasingly set in my ways, I fully believed that my thoughts and emotions were based on objective truths. I also never bothered to ask myself, *If I'm so smart, why am I so unhappy?*

During my seven years in the Pathwork, I'd directed most of my time and energy toward uncovering and releasing my negative emotions. By the time I reached my early fifties, I'd felt as though I was sailing in calmer waters—no longer tossed and turned by the stormy oceans of my long-repressed emotions. Nonetheless, deep down, I still felt in conflict with both myself and the world at large. I was plagued by a nagging inner hunger I didn't know how to appease.

After leaving the Pathwork, I made it my priority to closely observe my thoughts and behavior. I began to notice that my mind functioned as a storehouse for all my memories, beliefs, and emotions. Although it felt as if I was constantly having fresh experiences, more often than not, I was thinking, feeling, and reacting to those experiences in predictable ways, as if I was on autopilot. Unconsciously, I was projecting memories from my storehouse onto the outside world.

From the day of my birth in Jaworzno, I'd been bombarded with data about who I was, what I should be like, and what was expected of me. All this information was deposited in my brain, as were all of the stones that had been thrown at me, each death I had witnessed, and every good-bye I had been forced to say.

My mind warehoused all this input in much the same way papers are stored in a filing cabinet, except for one big difference: with a physical filing cabinet, you can choose to only keep things of value; it's easy to throw out any old, useless material you find inside. I, unfortunately, didn't have that same freedom with the information filed away in my mind. As a result, my mind's behavior was automatic, keeping me trapped in a deep-rooted cycle of fear and pain. Despite all the work I'd done on myself, my old and unhappy script kept repeating itself, with no end in sight.

I was tired of it. I'd had enough pain for one lifetime.

—◊◊◊—

During this time of preoccupation with the workings of my mind, I bought my first computer. It was exciting. Computers were just being introduced to the general public, and I was the only person I knew to own one. I was completely fascinated by how it worked and everything it could accomplish so quickly.

The parallels I saw between the workings of the computer and the human brain were enlightening. In both cases, information gets inputted, stored, and then faithfully played back. Both can be programmed in any variety of ways.

Because of my habitual patterns, different thoughts or events triggered emotional responses at a rate similar to a high-speed computer—lightning-fast. It happened so quickly, in fact, that I usually acted on these emotions instantaneously and impulsively, even though doing so was often against my best interests. My analytical brain, in contrast, worked much more slowly, which is why my old patterns usually won out.

It became clear to me that I didn't control my thoughts. They controlled me. What's more, my thoughts seemed to have an intrinsic shrewdness and a will to dominate. They shared my innate human survival instinct and were driven to safeguard themselves for perpetuity.

As I began to realize how dysfunctional it was to consider my beliefs to be facts when in truth they were totally arbitrary, I asked myself: *If I'd been born into a different culture, would my values, world outlook, and personality be the same? What if I'd been born on a different continent, into a different race or religion? What if I'd been taller or shorter by eight inches? What would this "me" be like if I were to spend the next five years at sea or in the Gobi Desert?*

My thoughts were not my own, and often they told me lies, but still, I did their bidding.

When I was growing up, if my parents, family, and all my neighbors had limped on one leg, I would have done the same. Such is the power of imitation. By example, I'd been taught to judge others and be judged in return. I'd learned that I wasn't good enough. As a result, I was filled with anxiety, alienation, and dissatisfaction. Unfulfilled longings and unrealized goals were my way of life. I was trapped by my beliefs like an animal in a cage.

Looking back at my life, I can clearly see that people's thoughts attract and repel one another just like magnets, exerting a push and pull that keeps us in bondage. Thoughts are contagious, and the human race is receptive to a herd mentality. There is every reason to assume that if I'd been raised in a family and culture of murderers, I would have been just like them. Murder would have seemed natural because I wouldn't know another way. I hate to think what I might have been like if I'd been raised in Germany during the days of Hitler.

The power of beliefs to create good and evil should never be underestimated. Our beliefs become weapons we aim at other people and at ourselves. A threat to them can feel like a threat to our very lives. Just observe the willingness of so many people to blindly offer their lives in service of their beliefs.

We members of the human race are constantly fighting and inflicting the miseries of war upon one another. Today, we're even in danger of destroying our planet. Nothing can explain the horrors of human existence as much as our automatic, mechanical, and repetitive thinking, feeling, and acting.

As I grew to understand the depth, strength, and destructive tendencies of my slavish devotion to my thoughts, I became outraged and despairing. I felt as if there was a conspiracy going on throughout the world and I dare not stand idly by. Shouldn't humans be free to choose and shape our own destinies? I wanted to shout, loud and long enough for everyone to hear, "Please, let us learn to live in peace, grace, and dignity. Evolution is failing us. We must not be willing to live forever as slaves to our limited minds and antiquated belief systems!"

I began to wonder what the world would be like if children were given new tools with which to look at life. We can't eliminate all of the unconscious messages children get, but what if we taught them how the human mind works and how to keep from getting trapped by their own habit-forming behavior? If young people learned to take responsibility for their own thoughts and belief systems, it could save them a great deal of heartache and despair later on. They would also grow up more mature, understanding, and tolerant.

CHAPTER 24: THE FALLACY
OF PROGRESS

"Scientific breakthroughs abound, but we have yet to discover spiritual elevators that can lift us into a world of light and love."

After living in California for a little over a year, I had to go back to Manhattan to finish up some odds and ends related to selling my business. I flew into New York from San Francisco on an overnight flight that landed before dawn, then made my way to the corner of Wall Street and Broadway, where I had a 10:00 a.m. meeting. I was right in the middle of the financial district, but because I arrived so early, all the stores were still closed. There wasn't anything for me to do, so I took a seat on some steps and waited.

When the vendors opened for business, I bought a newspaper, coffee, and pastry, and returned to my spot on the steps. After a while, I got restless and began to walk around the block. In the meantime, the quiet, empty streets slowly got busier and noisier. Traffic gradually increased, coming and going from all directions. Cars and trucks sped by and honking filled the air.

Soon the sidewalks were overflowing with pedestrians; the morning rush hour in New York City had arrived. Suddenly, I realized that I was in the midst of a very interesting phenomenon: with brains and intelligence being used in such a mechanistic way, humans have created cultures—in fact, entire civilizations—that reflect and duplicate our inner state.

I lived in New York City for four decades, but I had been so caught up in the hustle and bustle that I'd failed to notice it before. It was only after moving to California that I could see the big city with fresh eyes. Distance and leisure had given me a new perspective, like a person from a small town visiting for the very first time.

Standing near the subway entrance, I could feel the ground trembling. Underneath the sidewalk, trains were coming to a halt to disgorge their passengers. I watched masses of humanity emerge. On the street, people of all ages proceeded into tall office buildings, ready to perform their daily ritual of putting in a day's work. Most looked affluent, energetic, and determined—but also mechanical.

They walked at a rapid pace, their faces absorbed in thought. I didn't notice anyone looking around to take in the world that surrounded them. Perhaps they were still thinking about unfinished business from the day before or were distracted by endless concerns about the future. Why didn't they consider this to be a brand-new day to live fully and enjoy?

In their respective offices, people knew what was expected of them. Their roles were prescribed by their employers and culture, as well as by their talents and psychological makeup. But beneath the veneer of good manners and cordiality, almost everyone was in an ongoing struggle for acceptance, promotion, and domination. Unfulfilled needs—including cravings for love, appreciation, power, security, and fame—clamored for attention.

Manhattan, when viewed from the sky above, looks similar to a beehive, especially during morning and evening rush hour, when more than a million people commute in and out of the city.

And just like the incredible behavior exhibited in a beehive, most human activities are so well programmed into our brains that we perform them automatically.

If bees could talk, they might insist that they pollinate flowers out of their own free will. While we know they don't have a choice in the matter, it's much harder for us to grasp that, more often than not, we aren't exercising free will either. Our conditioning forces us to live the majority of our lives on autopilot, subservient to the expectations of society in our day and age. All this was apparent as I sipped my coffee and observed.

I've often asked myself why the news is flooded with violence and why there's so much suffering, fear, and heartbreak in the world. Could it be that the brilliant human brain, the very intellect that took us to the moon, is also a destructive force, working against our own best interests psychologically, emotionally, and spiritually? Every inhumane act begins with a thought, and peoples' thoughts can sync, so that they pounce on their prey like a pack of wolves.

When it comes to the workings of the mind, we still live in the dark ages. Our demons are as old as history, and our inner world has hardly changed over the past centuries. Neither science, money, education, nor government has proved capable of eliminating fear, hate, greed, or indifference. We are no closer to true insights about how to deal with the dark side of our nature.

The "progress" we've achieved hasn't transformed the way we're trapped by thought patterns based on scarcity and fear. Advancements that have improved our physical lives haven't brought us any closer to peace of mind. Scientific breakthroughs abound, but we have yet to discover spiritual elevators that can lift us into a world of light and love.

For more than fifty years, thinking hadn't helped me solve the problems that stood in the way of my happiness. As long as

I continued to glorify my brain instead of learning to rise above my mechanical conditioning, I wouldn't be able to choose love over fear, or freedom over slavery.

I had finally uncovered my basic problem: I was so proud of my brain that I'd failed to recognize its shortcomings.

CHAPTER 25:

SEEKING SOLUTIONS

"Figuring out how to live joyously was the biggest riddle of my life."

Like everyone else, I was born innocent, with unlimited potential. I came into this world like a book with blank pages, and then a script was written that became my ongoing tale. Certain things were emphasized by the writers of my story—correct behavior, conformity, and the power of the intellect—while other things were ignored: the importance of peace of mind, inner freedom, and a love of nature. The unity of existence and my place in the cosmos was never addressed.

As my life unfolded, decade after decade, my outer circumstances changed dramatically, but my inner life remained more or less the same. Even as I got on in years, I continued to remain loyal to my script, and never bothered to ask why. Looking back, I wondered where all the years had gone. It seemed surreal, like a dream. In many ways, I was truly asleep, and just beginning to awaken from my slumber.

For most of my life, I had no clue that a new script was in order. I didn't even know there was a reason to ask for one or that I was allowed to make that request. But finally, I came to realize that I could and should figure out how to write a new story. It's never too late.

During this period of self-examination, I was fortunate to rediscover the teachings of Krishnamurti, a brilliant Indian writer, philosopher, and lecturer who spoke all over the world. I had read one of his books during my time in the Pathwork but hadn't found his writings relevant then. It was only now, years later, that Krishnamurti's philosophy triggered in me a new worldview—a novel look at the human scene from a broader, more spiritual perspective.

Krishnamurti's teachings addressed virtually all the questions I'd been grappling with for so long. He talked about the nature of our brain—how repetition is its forte, and how hard it is to break free from generations of being told how to think and what to do. He emphasized the importance of curiosity, observation, inquiry, and liberty, and explained the difference between true learning and the accumulation of knowledge.

Krishnamurti didn't consider any one nation to be his home. He didn't belong to any religious organization, and he spoke frequently about how religion often divides humanity, contributing to our conflicts. Krishnamurti cautioned people not to blindly follow any authority outside themselves, himself included. He spoke about how hard it is to live a life that isn't distorted by our projections, and made it clear why unhappiness, alienation, cruelty, and wars are so prevalent.

Krishnamurti's teachings sounded simple at first, but they weren't at all easy to put into practice. My ego's greatest fear was abandonment, and it didn't appreciate coming under scrutiny. My old patterns thrived in darkness and wanted to avoid the light. Figuring out how to live joyously was the biggest riddle of my life, and Krishnamurti's insights were a powerful beacon for me.

Krishnamurti was so important to me that in the summer of 1980, our family traveled to Gstaad, Switzerland, so I could hear him speak. A few years later, on the only leisure trip I'd taken alone since marrying Edith, I went to Ojai, California, to be near him again. I came home with a suitcase full of his books and cassette tapes I listened to again and again.

—ᏪᏪ—

In my own internal journey, an unending reservoir of conflicts still needed to be resolved. The going was slow and the process was arduous. But simultaneously, shifts were beginning to take place at deeper levels of awareness. My consciousness of self-pity, resentment, and cold indifference were beginning to give way to a gentler, more cheerful reality.

I began to notice that even though I didn't always get what I *wanted*, I usually got what I *needed*. With this knowledge, my perception of the world began to change. I became more receptive to a universe that was congenial and pleasing—one I couldn't understand with my physical senses and intellect alone.

A transformation was beginning to take root in my psyche. At times when I least expected it, the gates of my internal fortress opened to green meadows and pastures of endless calm. I experienced moments of spontaneous joy and wonder over the freshness of a rainy day or the beauty of a flower. Ordinary things that had previously held only utilitarian value—houses on the street, cars on the roads, people walking around—appeared vivid and dazzling. The whole of nature revealed its secrets to me, and once again I could feel the pure joy I'd first experienced in Arosa. Everything I saw or heard was no longer isolated from anything else. There was a unity to life and I was part of it.

My growing awareness of the strength of love and goodness in the universe was revolutionary for me. Just the possibility that I could, in fact, be living in a safe and affectionate world was in itself a partial liberation.

These happy, peaceful moments provided a respite from the dreariness that still lived within me. Intermittent experiences of a joyous cosmos—sporadic realizations that love is a powerful adhesive that holds the world together—gave me a taste of how wonderful it could feel to be alive. These experiences showed me that there was far more to this life than just what my analytical brain could perceive or explain. They gave me a new optimism and made me want to learn how to live in a benevolent world full time.

I began writing about these events—the beauty I saw and how peaceful and joyous I felt—and through writing, I experienced them all over again. The more I read what I'd written, the happier I felt. Clearly, changing the type of information I put into my mechanical brain was altering its output. I began to feel calm, connected, and joyous more often.

The benefits of thinking positive thoughts were immediate, which inspired me to feed myself a steady diet of them. Throughout the day, whenever positive affirmations popped into my head, I'd write them down on scraps of paper. Afterwards, I'd read them again and again to imprint them in my mind and flood my body with joy. They didn't need to be especially profound—the only criterion they had to meet was that they made me feel good.

One day I wrote, "Now is a good time to be cheerful. There is never a good time to be fearful." Another day: "There is joy within me, I smile with it," and, "I pick that which is loving and kind. I want all that is delightful and celebrates life." Over time, I wrote hundreds of affirmations. Wherever I went, my pockets were full of these papers. My goal was to change my script to one filled with love, freedom, and adventure—a new life story that I would be eager to embody.

Positive affirmations were a very effective tool, but after a while I knew the time had come to voyage still deeper. For this next step in my healing journey, I turned to something that had always come very naturally to me: my imagination.

CHAPTER 26: VISUALIZATION

"I was able to plant flowers in my mind where formerly only weeds had grown."

Ever since I was a little boy in Poland, some form of visualization has been an active, indispensable part of my life. I'd learned by trial and error that diverting my attention from my unhappy life to a world of imagination brought me comfort and relief. My father might vent his fury on me on Saturdays, but for the rest of the week, instead of worrying, I could fantasize myself into a better world. Daydreaming was my answer to an unacceptable reality.

In my imagination, I could be strong, accomplished, and loved. Sometimes I imagined myself confidently riding an enormous, handsome brown horse that was my trusted friend. Together, we explored faraway villages and had a magical time. The wind against my face felt delightful as we swiftly galloped through the beautiful countryside.

My daydreams nourished images of hope and success. As I grew into manhood, these images generated an excitement within me that urged me onward to fulfill my destiny. I don't think I could have survived more than a thousand days of the extreme cruelty, starvation, and hard labor I experienced in the concentration camps without daydreaming. Even in the worst of times, through my daydreams, I was able to visualize new possibilities for myself. When people ask me how I stayed alive during the war, I often answer, "Visualization."

Later in my life, visualization was essential to my success in business. Before I could build a machine, I had to design it in my mind. I'd picture different combinations of complex mechanical and electrical parts interacting with each other into a workable whole, and I'd keep the visions alive in my head as the concepts blossomed and matured. I stubbornly held on to these ideas through thick and thin, even though they didn't always manifest the desired results right away.

During all the years I experimented with different psychological approaches to ease my pain, visualization was always a good, dependable friend. Like nothing else, visualization brought me the realization that life is neither fixed nor limited, but rather an ever-changing opportunity for exploration and wonder. It freed me to experience a brighter future and no longer feel like a helpless bystander. When I count my blessings, visualization is always high on my list. I can't imagine what my life would have been like without the ability to dream.

—◆—

It was those long-ago sessions with the hypnotherapist in Brooklyn that inspired me to begin to daydream once again as a middle-aged man. The therapist used guided imagery to introduce positive ideas with the goal of influencing my perceptions, emotions, and behavior. The results were immediate, albeit short-lived. For a few hours after each session, I was able to enjoy a wonderful feeling of calm and general optimism—until it was wiped away by my old habits that refused to give way. That feeling was akin to the freedom I had felt while daydreaming as a child.

Some nights, when I was too disturbed to fall asleep, I'd remember Arosa. I'd picture myself joyously and gracefully gliding down the shimmering white slopes, surrounded by beautiful mountains and happy people. Soon, I'd gently drift off into a deep slumber.

Other times, such as when I was waiting to catch the subway on my way to work on a dreary day, I'd imagine myself exploring the beautiful countryside or resting peacefully on the banks of a flowing river. The next day I'd recall the experience and expand upon it, enjoying it once again.

Once, while walking on a deserted street alongside an old cemetery in Brooklyn, I found myself imagining that Frank Sinatra had invited me to attend a special gala affair at which famous celebrities would be in attendance. This spontaneous, novel daydream took me by surprise. My mind was behaving in a way that was strange to me, forming visions so unfamiliar that I felt as if the brain in my head might belong to a different person altogether.

My old patterns weren't maintaining their usual strict control—my defenses were loosening up as my imagination was unleashed. Inadvertently, I was educating myself to look at the world differently, in a way that brought me peace and joy.

At this new crossroads in my life, I became committed to using visualization as one of my primary techniques for retraining my mind. I realized that the origin of the information being fed into my brain really didn't make a difference. Whether the input was an actual experience, an old memory, or a novel fantasy, my emotional responses were consistent and predictable: happy thoughts made me feel happy, and disturbing thoughts caused worry and upset. Therefore, my plan was to build an inventory of new, joyful thoughts and experiences in the same way I'd have learned how to play the piano: through practice and repetition.

Once I let go of the idea that it was immature for a grown man to spend his time frolicking in a world of fantasy, I had no inhibitions. Since no one could see what was going on in my head, I allowed myself to become a child all over again, to be as foolish and outrageous as I wanted. I enjoyed floating on clouds and riding magic carpets to the farthest corners of the universe. I played with magic hoops, throwing them high into the sky, where they filled the heavens with color and merriment before returning to me and gently curling around my neck. I invented new civilizations where I imagined myself befriending fascinating, undiscovered tribes. I explored the world as a tiny, invisible being, and also as a fearless, self-assured, ten-foot-tall giant.

For years, my favorite visualization was of a cathedral situated way up high on the very top of a tall mountain in a world that was made only of color. Nothing existed but color, myself included. Any words I uttered came out of my mouth as different hues. I loved to simply stand in this glorious cathedral, feeling bathed in a sea of delight and tranquility. I knew there was nothing else for me to do, nowhere else I needed to go. The silence, loveliness, and grace mesmerized me. The cathedral represented divine attributes buried deep within me, and I visited often.

Visualization also helped me face and overcome my insecurities, fears, and depressions. I created an exercise where I imagined that I was living alone in a cave, hiding from the world. I was afraid to leave because monster-like creatures were waiting for me outside. Eventually, I'd get tired of living such a wretched, isolated existence and realize I couldn't forever stand passively by, letting others decide my fate. I'd resolve to make my exit and fight desperately for my life. In this scenario, I always won, but surprisingly, my newfound freedom always felt painful. Even in my imagination, I couldn't take it for long and would eventually return to my miserable existence in the cave—but after a time, I'd fight my way out once more. I repeated this process over and over again, until I was finally able to feel comfortable being free.

One of the most valuable benefits of my visualizations were that they often saved me from being at the mercy of my negative thought patterns. Yet there were still times when I was feeling down, bewildered, or was expecting the worst, and was unable to visualize successfully. My mind was hooked on an unpleasant scenario that blocked everything else out. When this happened, I had to bide my time and wait for the storm to blow over. This was especially true in the beginning, when my brain was still open country, and negative thoughts and emotions roamed freely.

—m—

For many years, I believed I'd be able to uncover a simple answer to the riddle of the mind. Perhaps my success as an inventor had made me overconfident. Back then, I didn't fully understand how much my desire to change would threaten my ego, whose primary job was to preserve the total conglomerate of my beliefs, worldview, and personality.

Luckily, visualizing proved to be my Trojan horse—I was able to sneak my visualizations into my mind while staying under the radar of my ever-vigilant ego. They managed to bypass the resistance of my ingrained doubts and habits, and eventually enabled me to plant flowers in my psyche where formerly only weeds had grown.

The benefits of visualization came about so slowly that sometimes I doubted its efficacy. It was like adding new rooms to an old house—the old house remained intact and was only slightly changed by the new additions. Initially, I wasn't ready to move into the new rooms because I was more comfortable living in squalor, away from the sunshine and fresh air. But I kept building them, adding new wings and a new landscape, until there was enough of this "new me" to eclipse the old. After many years, as the content of my thoughts changed, I began to feel welcomed into the new rooms. The world became brighter and my heart began to fill with joy and wonder.

CHAPTER 27: MY SANCTUARY

"To the north, there was a road that stretched out to infinity. This road represented the enigma of life—the puzzle of creation."

The most desirable piece of real estate I ever owned was a place located on a plateau in the midst of a beautiful mountain range, and it never cost me a cent. I called it "my sanctuary," and it was a place of rest and leisure where the health of my body and the well-being of my mind were restored and invigorated. This sanctuary was one of my most often used visualizations. With time, it became as real, perhaps even more so, as any place I had ever inhabited.

My sanctuary had a large, oval lake fed by a waterfall that originated from the snow-covered mountains above. Its crystal-clear water was so transparent that you could see all the way to the bottom. The water temperature was comfortable—slightly cooler in the morning, a little warmer in the afternoon—and always inviting and soothing. Wrapped around the lake were gardens overflowing with beautiful, fragrant flowers, softly sloping hills, and tall trees that reached up toward the heavens. The trees stood ever upright, guarding my sanctuary from the countless negative thought forms floating around on earth.

Resting on the velvety green pasture, soothed by the sounds of the waterfall rushing down the mountainside, my mind went silent. Bathed in the healing powers of nature, I watched the tall trees swaying softly in the breeze against the clear blue sky as the sun warmed my body. I was at peace, protected not only from the constant strife and confusion pervading the "real world" but also from fear itself.

No apples, pears, or apricots ever tasted as sweet as they did in my sanctuary. I never tired of the flower garden, and the waterfall was always a source of childlike delight. I could choose the color of the water at will, and I alternated it to match my mood. As I stood underneath the cascade and allowed the fresh water to run over my body, I was cleansed of all my sins, doubts, and fears.

Between the forest and the gardens was a small, round house with large windows framing magnificent views. The entire home was a simply furnished bedroom that blended harmoniously with the outdoors. Special hinges on the large, red oak doors enabled them to move with only the slightest touch of a finger. Despite their massive weight, the doors opened and closed as if they were floating on air.

To the north, there was a road stretching out to infinity that I knew I must inevitably walk one day. This road represented the enigma of life, the puzzle of creation. I had no idea where it went, but I knew it would lead somewhere wonderful.

The only people I invited into my sanctuary were my wife and daughters. Edith was a frequent visitor. Holding hands, we would walk the grounds and appreciate the beauty all around us. Ruthie and Myra loved to swim in the lake and were fascinated by the monkeys in the forest. The waterfall was their favorite.

The more I visited my sanctuary, the sharper the focus and the more intense the experience. After many happy years, it became a part of my consciousness and an extension of myself.

My sanctuary is still very much alive in me now. I think about it with pleasure and satisfaction, returning to it whenever my needs or fancy take me there.

I suspect that my sanctuary exists on some level of reality that cannot be explained—a place that is open to the public, where everyone is welcome.

CHAPTER 28:

REMEMBERING FREEDOM

"I had walked upright with dignity and confidence."

My visualizations helped me shift my thoughts and energy toward the positive and experience a more joyous universe. They also gave me the tools and fortitude to tackle my past, which was the necessary next step in healing my deepest wounds. In order to give up fear as a way of life, I knew I had to face my history and get a fresh perspective on the boy I'd once been.

When I first tried to remember my life as a little boy, my mind would go blank. It was as if a thick fog had descended over my past, obscuring it and preventing me from finding my way back. I felt like an unwelcome stranger in my own house.

For my entire adult life, my childhood had been off limits—a secret, forbidden region I dared not enter. I was terrified to remember my boyhood in Jaworzno and had blocked almost all of those memories. The few I had retained were virtually all grim, which only served to reinforce my unhappiness. Instead of making an effort to remember the good, I had spent my life feeling sorry for myself. Dwelling on the negative had become an addiction, one as difficult to overcome as a drug user's habit.

Going back in time to relive events that had taken place so long ago was extremely arduous, especially in the beginning. As I accessed my childhood memories and began to write them down, I went through a million difficult feelings. It really shook me up. Fortunately, however, in addition to the bleak memories I began to recall some delightful ones, which felt like uncovering buried treasure.

I was surprised to discover that I'd completely forgotten about so many good experiences. Each time I recalled something pleasant, I'd welcome and cherish those newfound gems. I thought of them over and over, feeding my mind and heart until they became indelibly impressed into my consciousness.

In my search for positive experiences, I regularly brought myself back in time to the places I'd enjoyed in Jaworzno. I conjured up the people I'd loved, the taste of my favorite foods, and the activities that had once delighted me. I remembered the good deeds I'd performed and recollected my youthful hopes and dreams. These flashbacks quickly became a source of pleasure, security, and inspiration. They also provided me with raw material for future visualizations.

The most wonderful childhood experience I remembered was a three-week vacation I took with three of my cousins to a little mountain resort town in Poland called Jordanuv. Like an oasis in the desert, that trip to Jordanuv was an experience of freedom, adventure, and joy that stands out against an otherwise frustrating, painful, and dreary childhood.

I was only seven or eight at the time of this magical vacation. After weeks of begging, nagging, and manipulating, my mother finally gave me the green light to join my cousins on this excursion. I don't know whether it was out of love or weakness, or a combination of the two, but my mother not only said yes, she also managed to persuade my father to give his blessing.

My three young cousins and I were entrusted to a "very reliable" chaperone that would look after our welfare, a young man from our hometown who happened to be going to Jordanuv as well. The truth is, he was a happy-go-lucky, easygoing chap who couldn't care less what we did. Not once did he bother to inquire how we were or what we were doing with all of our free time. I was overjoyed.

Those three weeks were the first time in my life I spent time away from home. It was also the first time I traveled by train, and the first time I didn't have to worry about school. But more than that, it was the only time in my childhood when I was able to just *be* for an extended period of time. From the moment we got on the train, I felt like a bird let out of a cage. For hours, I looked out the window, spellbound. I was surprised at how the moving landscape continually ran away from me in the opposite direction.

When we arrived at the station, our chaperone hired a carriage with two horses to bring us to our hotel. As we made our way slowly through the cobblestone streets, the cart bounced up and down until my bones got sore and my stomach hurt, but nothing could dampen my enthusiasm. Along the way, we passed the town square and a marketplace buzzing with activity.

Our accommodations might have been considered meager. All four of us had one tiny attic room to share, and there was nothing in the room but four straw beds and some blankets. Due to the structure of the roof, the room inside looked like a triangular box, and we had to constantly watch not to bump our heads against the wall. But who cared? We were free!

I was thrilled to be in this little town and intoxicated by my unlimited free time. How liberating to go to bed every night with the knowledge that tomorrow I didn't have to give an account to anyone. We were served three meals a day with snacks in between. Nothing was asked of me, and my soul soared high.

The people of Jordanuv were relaxed and easygoing. An atmosphere of gaiety pervaded the place. In the far corner of the marketplace, children played and danced in the streets. I was surprised by all the festivity. I'd never seen children who were permitted to have so much fun.

I also savored the fact that Jordanuv was apparently free from anti-Jewish bias. Dressed in Hasidic garments with locks showing below my ears, I looked like all the Jewish boys from my hometown—nothing like the local population. But in Jordanuv, no one seemed to notice that I stood apart.

It was as if I had discovered a whole new world.

Over the next three weeks, I was an explorer in a foreign land. There was a little river in the nearby forest. I loved to gaze at it and listen to its soothing sounds. I roamed the marketplace and other parts of town for hours on end. I was a wanderer, drifting without cares or obligations, consumed with curiosity and wonder. In the safety and freedom of my own being, I walked about from place to place aimlessly, without a trace of fear or embarrassment. It was enough for me to be alive, to mingle with the farmers bringing their produce to market and the horse and cattle traders who came to town from the surrounding villages.

On the way from the hotel to the marketplace, I had to cross a bridge that overlooked a huge gypsy camp that occupied the banks of the river below. Every time I passed the bridge, curiosity got the better of me: I'd stop for a while, lean against the railing, and observe a community of people who had a way of life unlike anything I'd ever seen before.

Their mode of living fascinated me. They cooked their meals outdoors and slept in tents. The children were always outside playing. There was no school or *cheder* for them. *How lucky they are*, I thought, jealousy rushing through my veins. They might have been poor and dressed in rags, but I would have happily traded places with them.

Although I was only in Jordanuv for a few weeks, my time there taught me what it was like to roam freely without feeling other people's hatred and prejudice directed at me. I had experienced carefree laughter. I had walked upright with dignity and confidence, unencumbered by the restrictions, habits, and customs of my upbringing.

—ɱ—

Remembering my liberating adventure in Jordanuv led me to recall another place where I'd experienced pure freedom: a place that I called the Hidden Valley of the Fields. It was located right in my hometown, behind the biggest synagogue we had—the one where I went to study the Talmud. A five-foot rock wall separated the synagogue from the farmland behind it, where the local farmers cultivated wheat and corn.

The fields went on and on, as far as the eye could see. As kids, we'd scale the wall, jump to the other side, and find ourselves in what felt like a different world. We never tired of hanging out in these fields on our days off from school. But what I loved the most was going there alone, whiling away the hours in solitude.

For me, the separation between town and the fields was more than physical. With nothing but wheat, corn, and the blue sky above, nothing disrupted the internal calm of the land. Once I scrambled over the wall, I was out of reach of the long arm of the law—society's unwritten code for proper behavior. Far from the jurisdiction and obligations of my culture, religion, and upbringing, I found silence, freedom, and peace.

To get to my special spot, I had to pass through the narrow paths between the tall stalks of corn and wheat. Situated amidst the stalks, entirely hidden from view, was a huge, hollow, bowl-like crater, five or six feet deep. It appeared to me that this valley had been created for a purpose—that it was patiently waiting for someone to make good use of it. So, I did. I went there as often as I could.

Some days I'd sit on the grass and do nothing. Other days, I'd run up the valley's steep walls and then quickly turn and run back down again, unless I tumbled down the hill. Even when I got tired and felt I'd had enough, I'd keep running some more, until, utterly exhausted, I'd collapse on the grass, happy, sleepy, and dreamy.

The Hidden Valley seemed to be the only safe place on earth. I felt like even God couldn't reach me there. Far from the world of men and the magnetic field of human thought, I could momentarily release my defensive posture and drop my guard.

Alone in my Hidden Valley, I experienced a timeout otherwise missing from my life. Every time I went there, I felt a deep satisfaction just being alive. I felt wanted, loved, protected, and accepted. I had the world all to myself and could do whatever I pleased.

It was in the safety of this special place that I first allowed my imagination to soar. Those images I created as a boy were like magic seeds planted in the ground, waiting for the right time to germinate. Lying in the tall grass, I sent visions of love and freedom into the universe—thoughts of better times to come that were never extinguished.

CHAPTER 29: EMBRACING MY INNER CHILD

"When I love and accept every part of myself just as I am, I'm as close to perfection as I will ever be."

When I pointed my telescopic lens on that little boy alone in the Hidden Valley of the Fields, I became cognizant of many things about myself that would otherwise have escaped my attention. What I saw was a scared child full of anger and resentment—a boy who craved love, security, and acceptance. He felt lost, shy, and overwhelmed by life, and had a sense of desperation not unlike a cornered animal with no hope of escape. He was ashamed of his inadequacies and his needs, yet he was also stubborn and proud, refusing to admit, even to himself, that he was hurting.

As I spent more time with this boy, I could feel him waking up inside of me. I could see that his need for free expression, love, play, and self-respect were valid, and that even his hurt and rage had been warranted. As a child, I couldn't possibly understand that I'd been entombed by the pressures of a culture and time in history not conducive to my well-being, or that I never should have been required to repress my joy or my sorrow.

For most of my life, I'd never really liked the little child within me, and no wonder. I didn't want to be a persecuted Jewish boy from Poland who was afraid of his own shadow. Why should I want to bother with him? Little Mendek's needs, insecurities, and fears posed a danger to my peace of mind. He threatened the artificial self-image I had created for myself.

I'd thought I was simply ignoring him, when in fact my adult self and my child self had been afraid of one another. I'd spent my time here on earth not listening to my heart, even though it was almost breaking.

When I finally understood that learning to love Little Mendek was a prerequisite to healing my pain, I stopped avoiding his gaze and looked at him with a new interest. I quickly grew to admire his curiosity, mechanical aptitude, and sense of wonder. I delighted in his ability to abandon himself unreservedly to life, love, and joy—a capacity that had lain dormant in me for many decades but had never been completely extinguished.

Even though I had flunked public school and my father had beaten me for my failures in *cheder*, I had never been a "bad" child. The circumstances surrounding me had just been unfortunate. Once I understood this, I decided once and for all that I'd never again reject, ignore, or feel ashamed of Little Mendek in any way. I would accept and love him unconditionally.

In my imagination, I began looking deeply at Little Mendek. I reached out to hold his hand and told him, "No matter what, I will always accept you exactly as you are. I will never limit you in any way." I comforted him by saying, "It's alright to be afraid. Everyone is scared sometimes." I held him close and felt his pain. With great compassion I reassured him, "It's okay to be wrong sometimes. I promise that I will always forgive you. Please forgive me, too."

I began to converse with myself facing a mirror, asking my child self the following questions, one at a time: "Have I been good to you lately? Have I been your best friend and strongest ally? Do I demand too much from you? How can I appreciate you more? How can I become a better friend?" Then I'd wait patiently until I heard my answer.

—◊◊◊—

I'd learned duality at a very young age—right versus wrong, beautiful versus ugly—and from then on, my mind had never been at rest. I believed that I had to prove myself worthy to deserve love and happiness, and the world began to feel like a threatening place. When I was told to be "good," I was afraid of being "bad." These opposing ideas battled inside of me continuously, and my heart grew less open to love. Locked inside the prison of society's expectations, my inner freedom all but disappeared.

I had accepted as fact that I should be different from who I naturally was, and as a result my innate spontaneity had given way to control. My moment-to-moment joys had been overtaken by a complicated, artificial structure created by my mind. Slowly but surely, my birthright had been usurped.

What I came to understand is that when I love and accept every part of myself just as I am, I'm as close to perfection as I will ever be. Uncovering this truth was perhaps the most important breakthrough I've ever had.

I decided that I would no longer make the mistake of looking to the past, with its insecurities and anxieties, as my reference points for the future. I wanted to live in the present and have the freedom and joy of a child again.

As I learned to cherish my inner child and integrate him with my adult self, I began to feel safer living in this world. Instead of being two lonely orphans who behaved like wary strangers, Little Mendek and I became friends. With him as my ally, my tortured heart began to heal and expand. For the first time, my past and present felt like they were merging together, forming one life in which I felt comfortable living.

Without my inner child, life had been a dreary affair; I'd lacked both roots to my past and enthusiasm about my future. The years I had denied the child within me were like a wasteland where nothing blossomed.

Over time, as I was able to fully embrace the little boy in me, I became a different person. It was the child in me who had always held my essential nature. Although I had forgotten, repressed, and denied this truth for so long, I'd come to this earth with the gift of freedom and the memory of the spark of the divine. That's why the little boy in me had always refused to accept life as merely the struggle to cope and survive.

—m—

Magic was something I believed in as a child but had given up as a matter of course as I grew up. I just didn't think it made sense anymore. But as I embraced my inner child, I found myself playing with the word "magic" like a child plays with a toy. As the word grew inside of me, "magic" became one of my favorite concepts. I wanted to rediscover it and reclaim it as my own.

Young children have a love of life and an unguarded innocence that gives them the ability to sense magic and see this world as a large playground filled with beauty and wonders to explore. As my long-forgotten, childlike faith began to resurface, I was able to sense magic all around me. Magic is the mystical formula that makes the sum greater than its parts. It is the reaching out for the unknown, no matter how impossible it may seem.

Finally, I understood that I needed to bow in reverence to the little boy in me, not the other way around. My inner child helped me begin to trust my heart more than I trusted my mind. Only then could I stop believing in the limited world I saw through the eyes of my conditioning, and finally experience marvels beyond what my five senses could perceive or my brain could explain. Welcoming magic was my joyful opening to life's countless mysteries.

CHAPTER 30: RE-ENVISIONING
MY WORLD

"I was free to choose the nature of the inner world I would inhabit."

When my mother was pregnant with me, I'm sure she and my father looked forward to my arrival with both glee and nervous anticipation. My birth was cause for celebration. As their first-born son, I was the answer to their prayers. My parents expected me to grow up to uphold their values and be a source of pride and satisfaction. When they reached old age, I would be a pillar of strength for them.

Yet underneath the rejoicing, there must have also been a sense of foreboding. As a Jew in Poland, I was destined to live a life of indignity and struggle. I was born to a people who had been uprooted from their homeland for two thousand years yet still managed to keep their traditions intact. They had both a history of victimhood and an unshakable belief in their sacred destiny—a deep faith in God and a deep distrust of life. I was born into a spider web of antiquity, thousands of years' worth of accumulated ideas, beliefs, and traditions.

How bewildering it must have been for me to come out of the peace and security of my mother's womb into a world of such dissonant thoughts and emotions. By the process of osmosis, I breathed in my people's history, assimilating it into my tender mind and body. I'd come from a place of infinite love where happiness was free, and arrived in an alien world of intellect and ideas where happiness had to be earned and deserved. I thought I was coming home, only to find myself stranded in a foreign land.

No one in my family saw me as a child of the universe. My parents looked at me through the eyes of their conditioning and believed that I belonged to them. They were certain they knew what was best for me. Soon, my original innocence and joy were eclipsed by my inheritance, layer upon layer of beliefs about what was right and wrong. I absorbed these deep, ancient fears like a dry sponge dropped in water.

In my quest to heal my emotional wounds, I sensed the importance of actually experiencing what it would have been like to grow up surrounded by freedom and joy. Thus I decided to use my imagination to recreate my past, making it as healthy and happy as I'd always wished it had been.

In my mind's eye, I went back in time to create a new and better world. I reinvented my parents as people who walked the earth fearlessly, feeling a happiness that stemmed from love and laughter. Just as he had been in real life, my father was strong, intelligent, and resourceful, but now he was also witty, gentle, and kind. My mother, who had always been wonderful in so many ways, was now also buoyant, filled with a joy she couldn't contain, as she danced and sang around our kitchen, cooking my favorite foods. How she adored me!

I visualized my parents loving each other intensely, having the freedom and courage to live the life they wanted to live. They easily embraced, held hands, and laughed. My mother and father played with me, and the three of us took much delight in each other's company. Together, we explored a world full of magic. There was nothing to fear.

Methodically, I watched a new and more delightful version of my life unfold. First, I imagined myself as a newborn, utterly secure and peaceful as I was lovingly held in my mother's arms. Then I was a delighted one-year-old, taking my first steps and saying my first words. Eventually, I was a cheerful five-year-old going off to my first day of school. All the while, I saw myself happily surrounded by all the people I loved the most.

I continued to watch myself develop into a teenager, having good times with friends, meeting my first girlfriend. I kept growing older, stronger, and more confident, until one day I knew I was ready to accept responsibility for my own life.

Through this process of re-envisioning, I confirmed that my past, no matter its travails, was not etched in stone. It did not have to remain fixed and stagnant, because I had the power to create a new and better yesterday imbued with all the positive emotions I'd always desired. I was free to choose the nature of the inner world I would inhabit.

Now, I choose to remember Jaworzno during the springtime. I can still see the early morning sun as it filtered its way through wild chestnut trees and into the windows of our house. The world is full of sunshine—a grand and happy place.

CHAPTER 31: A NEW LIGHT

"I was finally able to see that my childhood had never been devoid of love and joy."

Through the process of remembering and re-envisioning my life, my perception of my childhood and family changed. As I looked through new eyes that sought out everything good, I started to remember more tender moments, and times of gladness and laughter. Things stopped appearing as bleak as they once had, and I was finally able to see that my childhood had never been devoid of love and joy.

I also began to realize that when I was young, I didn't believe that I, a weak little boy, could hurt an adult. I was oblivious to the fact that I blamed my father for my unhappiness, thinking it was entirely his fault, and withdrew from him as a way to punish him. Since he didn't love or care for me in the way I wanted him to, I rejected his love altogether.

Eventually, my consciousness opened up enough to recollect things about my father that made me see him in a new light—memories that I'd managed to block for most of my life. Even though he'd never expressed his warm feelings directly, I began to remember times he'd showed his affection indirectly. He'd give me five *groshen* every day—the equivalent of 25 cents—to buy candy, peanuts, or a slice of salami that I liked very much. He even showed me his trust by letting me go to the money counter to take the money out by myself.

There was a beggar in our town who went from door to door. She always left us five dried beans to show her gratitude for our charity. My father knew I loved those beans, so he always put them in a special place for me so I could find them later on.

As a child, I assumed my father had no feelings and that nothing could affect him. How surprised I was when I burst into my parents' bedroom one day and found him crying like a baby, tears streaming down his face. He had just been notified of his mother's death.

Early on, in my first concentration camp, when we were still allowed to get mail from home, I received a few letters from my father. In them, I could sense his deep concern for me. But it wasn't until decades later, when I had children of my own, that I could understand the despair in my parents' hearts when they saw me for the last time as a prisoner under guard, walking toward the railroad station to an unknown destination. They didn't know what fate would befall me. At last, my heart went out to them.

In the past, when I'd tried to forgive my father, I'd only succeeded to a small extent because my heart wasn't fully open to him. But when my thoughts and feelings finally became united, the miracle of healing came about without me even trying, and I could truly open my heart to him.

From my new vantage point, I was finally able to see my father in his true light, and feelings of compassion and understanding flowed out of me toward him. I could now accept the truth I'd formerly chosen to deny: my father had loved me and I had loved him. Such is the miracle of life.

PART IV:

The World of Wonder

CHAPTER 32: CHOOSING
THE WORLD I WANT TO SEE

"No matter how troubled the outer world appears to be, I have the power to decide that a loving universe will exist for me."

I believe that life is a school and we are all put here on earth to grow in wisdom, love, and joy. It's inconceivable to me that humans are meant to suffer indignities and die in vain. The truth is, suffering can serve a higher purpose: it can be the stimulus that motivates us to change.

When I first began my healing journey, my pain was what motivated me to try to move away from a life filled with fear and alienation. I'd made a good deal of progress living more joyfully and peacefully, but it wasn't until I had a huge epiphany soon after we moved to California that I was able to make a dramatic shift.

One day, I heard myself repeating the sentence, *I choose to believe. I choose to believe. I choose to believe.* And I wondered . . . could it really be as simple as that? Could it really be that no matter how troubled the outer world appears to be, I have the power to decide that a loving universe will exist for me?

All of a sudden, I was certain that the answer was yes! If I could genuinely trust that life would provide me with everything I needed for my peace and well-being with the same conviction I'd always believed in struggle and unhappiness, my life would be transformed.

That's when I made one of the most pivotal decisions of my life—a decision that I would have to make not just once, but many times over: to always have faith in the limitless power of love.

—◊—

Faith did not come naturally to me. But once I understood that my thoughts, emotions, and actions were all determined by my beliefs, I decided to select my beliefs first and trust that the rest would follow. Since I couldn't fully believe in the omnipotent power of love just yet, I began by pretending to believe.

Letting go of my old belief system was difficult. I feared that without it, all that would remain was emptiness. I worried that I might even lose my mind altogether.

Nonetheless, I designed a series of exercises to train my mind to think in a new way and to open myself to faith. I discovered that I was more receptive to inquiries than statements, so I created the following list of questions to help me access my inner knowledge. I kept this list by my bedside, and asked myself these questions over and over again for many years:

1. *Do I believe that I am surrounded by an intelligence and wisdom greater than my own?*
2. *Do I believe that I am surrounded by a love and goodness greater than my own?*
3. *In spite of what I see and hear, do I believe that a spark of the divine lives in all humans?*
4. *Do I believe that I am as important to the cosmos as the cosmos is to me?*
5. *Do I believe that only within myself lives the potential for my total satisfaction?*

The act of asking mattered more than the answers, because sitting silently with the questions opened me up to new possibilities. My constantly churning thoughts—the ones that ran in circles all day long—couldn't possibly solve the problems that stood in the way of my happiness. The answers that arose from the source of love deep within me tapped into a far-reaching wisdom that was much greater than any human mind could produce.

—∿∿—

One morning, while flying home to California through Denver, I looked out the window from 25,000 feet in the air onto a world of magic. The sun was sending forth its bright rays of warmth, as if to gently awaken the whole planet from its slumber. When I observed closely, I had the uncanny feeling that the clouds and snowcapped mountains were conversing directly with me. Words were unnecessary. In that moment, I knew that everyone and everything communicates, that separateness is only an illusion invented by the intellect.

My beautiful view from the window contrasted sharply with the stories reported in *U.S. News and World Report* that the airline handed out to passengers to keep us entertained during the flight. Reading the magazine, it was easy to become despondent. Was the world running out of good and cheerful things to report? Acid rain was destroying whole forests in the United States and Western Europe, and behind the Iron Curtain. A stunning amount of pollution was causing a myriad of other problems. I wondered if it was only a matter of time before the earth would become unlivable.

For a while I was caught up in pessimistic thoughts about the human race. But then I remembered that my inner life determines my outer life, and the mind is the arena where conflicts originate and disharmony abides. So I made a conscious decision to stop focusing on the negative. I put the magazine down, returned my gaze to the glory outside, and was once again able to feel the full splendor of the sun shining down on me. In that moment,

I recognized that there is no place devoid of joy, love, or peace; it's just that negative thoughts can make something as strong and compelling as love impossible to see.

When my mind, heart, and soul choose that which is pleasant and good, I am sending messengers out into the world that make both me and the world more loving and joyful. This same principal holds true for my negative thoughts, so I try to be careful. I want my thoughts to be my friends—to add beauty and harmony to my life.

—⟋⟍—

One summer afternoon, I drove to the post office in Carmel and immediately found a parking space. This was a rarity, because it's a busy little town and I usually have to search for a long time. There was even an empty space next to mine, which was quickly taken by a lady who appeared to be in her mid-eighties. While I was mailing my letters, she walked over to me with a radiant smile and declared, "We are so lucky!"

Surprised, I asked why.

"Because we found such wonderful parking spaces!"

This woman's bright eyes and happy face stayed with me all day long. For a few hours, I kept repeating to myself, "I am so lucky! I am so lucky!" and almost immediately I began to see my good fortune everywhere. This woman with the unforgettable smile had given me a message from heaven: *Just believe you are lucky, and it will be confirmed.*

As I considered this, I saw that every time I should have died in the past, something happened to save my life. I'd gotten so many breaks—hundreds, if not thousands. All of a sudden, I realized that I was one of the luckiest guys alive.

CHAPTER 33: MY TRUE SELF

"My true Self doesn't have an age or an address. It has no past. It isn't Jewish. It doesn't build machines. It just is."

B eing retired in California gave Edith and me the opportunity to do things we'd never done before, like occasional gambling trips to Reno, Nevada. Our favorite game was five-card stud on slot machines. We played the nickel machines, so the most we could lose was twenty-five cents a shot—not a big risk, and we had a great time. We would sit on the stools for hours, gambling away, so absorbed that we were oblivious to the world outside.

Then, out of the blue, I had an experience that changed me forever.

While gambling one afternoon, I inadvertently caught a glimpse of myself in a mirror mounted on the wall beside me. What I saw was a person who looked like me but was very different from the person I perceived myself to be. This surprising reflection engaged my attention so strongly that everything else diminished in importance. The only way to describe it is that I became conscious of the fact that I am indeed a Self—a word that is still difficult for me to adequately explain.

This Self existed in a dimension of reality that was new to me, one beyond time and space. It was whole and perfect.

The Self I had just discovered transcended my proud little ego. No one could injure it or make it lose its equilibrium. While I could feel powerless, insecure, and helpless, it never did. It didn't experience fear, or share my needs, drives, or apprehensions. This Self was free from conflict, because its thoughts and actions were one. It had no wants besides just what *is*. Equanimity was its natural state of being.

Sitting there in front of the slot machine, I felt uplifted. How happy I would be if I could always be like this Self, forever connected to wisdom, confidence, and grace. I began wondering whether this being I had just encountered in the mirror was, after all, the "real me." Maybe the "me" I'd always identified with was just an artificial persona, a creation of my ego. My true Self is free from the human predicament. It doesn't have an age or an address. It has no past. It isn't Jewish. It doesn't build machines. It just is.

I felt as if this Self and I were two different people whose fates were intertwined—two faces on opposite sides of a coin. From a wider perspective, we were one, yet this Self was invincible, while I was not. I began to realize that my ego exists in time—in a world of fear and trepidation—while my true Self exists in eternity. If my daily life consists of pleasure and pain, the "good" and the "bad," my true Self exists in a perpetual state of bliss.

Although I'd never been aware of this Self when I was a little boy, it must have been my companion since the day I was born. It must have been with me in the coal mine when I stood there frozen with fear, watching the procession of Jews from my hometown. It must have been with me in the concentration camps.

And if this was true, I must also assume that the Jews I had witnessed on the walk were not alone. Their respective Selves were with them, too. I remembered the guards carrying machine guns on their shoulders. They were not alone, either. Then I thought of my parents standing in a gas chamber. They were not alone. Their Selves were with them, too. I shook my head in disbelief. I had to hold back my tears.

There I was, in a casino in Reno, having these strange, wonderful insights. I was so surprised by the complex emotions I was experiencing that I stopped gambling for a short while. When I began putting nickels in the machine again, I was no longer playing alone. I had invited the "other me" to join in the fun. I could feel that my newly discovered Self was smiling. Apparently, he had a great sense of humor.

For the next five or ten minutes, I was elated by this experience. I sensed a keen awareness of this "other me." It was wonderful to have acquired a new friend who felt like both a mentor and a protector. What a huge change to not be alone in the world!

It felt as if my luck had improved, because I kept winning. Then slowly, bit by bit, this happy interlude began to fade away. I continued gambling, but was no longer under the hypnotic power of my thoughts. Instead, I felt relaxed and free.

CHAPTER 34: BEING ME

"Loving myself, just as I am, is the most important act of kindness I can perform on this planet."

All my life, since I was a little boy, I've felt myself to be different from everybody else. The way I thought was definitely different. Except for math, learning was especially hard for me, while figuring out anything mechanical came inexplicably easily.

Overall, I felt inadequate and did everything I could not to draw attention to myself. I conformed. I didn't make waves. In my desperation to be accepted, I hid, even from myself, both the best and the worst parts of me. As the years passed, I learned to deny and repress almost all of my emotions.

My sister Bronia once told me that she'd always considered me odd growing up because I was so quiet and never complained or asked for much. She thought it was particularly strange that I insisted on mending my own socks, because sewing was considered to be a woman's job. But working with my hands and fixing broken things gave me pleasure and satisfaction. It felt empowering to darn my own socks instead of handing them over to my mother. And I was good at it.

As a child, sewing was one of those rare times I ignored prevailing customs and didn't worry about what people thought of me. Looking back, I'm happy I chose to do something that brought me pleasure rather than bowing to convention. I still enjoy darning my socks today, despite Edith's repeated encouragement to throw out the ones with holes and just buy new ones.

My most significant departure from convention was abandoning my Orthodox upbringing after the war. In America, I didn't eat kosher, observe *Shabbat*, or celebrate all the Jewish holidays. Despite the fact that I was mired in confusion and depression, I felt certain that the religion of my childhood wasn't the right road for me, and I listened to my inner voice.

Nonetheless, I'd spent much of the first forty or fifty years of my life giving my ego all the authority, without noticing that obeying its commands was getting me nowhere I wanted to be. When I sought happiness from the outside—by trying to gain other people's approval or by changing the circumstances of my life—I could never find it. Instead of contentment, my mind led me away from the source of my being, toward despair and loneliness.

My ego would say, "Don't make a fool out of yourself. People will think you're crazy!" So I suppressed the joy of life deep within me and lost touch with my true self. Occasionally, I'd get a glimpse of it, but I never felt safe enough to expose it for long. I wouldn't allow myself to laugh too loudly, hug a stranger out of sheer exuberance, or dance a jig. As humans, we're so well trained that if we don't watch ourselves, we end up doing what everyone else thinks is proper instead of what fulfills us. That's how our ego feels most comfortable.

It wasn't until I was well into middle age that I finally decided to stop wasting my energy seeking approval from others. Instead, I began to focus my resources on truly loving myself for who I was, moment by moment.

I stopped worrying about measuring up and gave myself the freedom to blunder. Letting go of my fear of failure made me more relaxed and joyous. The more I relinquished my ego's control over my life, the more I grew in wisdom and compassion. I began to feel certain that simply loving myself, just as I am, is the most important act of kindness I can perform on this planet.

The intention to love myself became my mantra. Upon awakening, I would say, "I love myself" over and over. I would feel this love expand within me, envelop me, nurture me, and keep growing stronger. I'd remember to say it as often as I could throughout the day—"I love myself, I love myself"—letting love flow through me, soothe me, strengthen me. The energy of boundless love felt so wonderful!

Then, as I got used to feeling this love in the morning, noon, and night, I began to feel it continuously, all day long. Soon I discovered that the more I loved myself, the more easily I could love others, and the more peaceful I became.

—m—

As a child, my uncle Yossele was the person I most admired. He was a man who followed his heart instead of looking to society for cues about how to behave. He brought peace and joy wherever he went, and always treated me, and everyone else, with kindness and respect.

My uncle Yossele was the only adult I knew who dared to be different, yet he was extremely well liked and respected. In my mind, he towered above other people in my hometown. This wasn't just because he was taller and more handsome than the other men. It was because he was extraordinary. Whenever I saw Yossele walking down the street or in the marketplace, something happened to me that I have no explanation for: I felt safe, and better about myself.

Yossele often came to our house for a meal and then stayed to tell stories about other parts of the world. When he started talking, I sat very still and listened to every word. I almost never spoke to Yossele, but I knew he did not judge me.

As a child, I often sat outside on the steps of my house, absorbed in thought or escaping into a world of daydreams. No one in my family was interested in what went on in my head, except for my uncle Yossele. Once he came over to me and said, "Tell me, Mendek, what you are thinking about and I will give you five *groshen*." He was curious enough to offer me a bribe, but I was too embarrassed to say.

Unlike everyone else, Yossele was not a strict follower of convention. While all the men went to the synagogue each morning during prayer time to pray, my uncle often arrived late. Yossele could also be seen in the marketplace on occasion, carrying pots of chicken soup to the sick, without showing any sense of embarrassment. This was unusual, because people usually sent their children on errands of this nature. It wasn't considered proper for a man to do this kind of thing.

Yossele always walked extremely slowly—deliberately so, it seemed to me. Wherever he went, he carried a sense of serenity and benevolence. He had no enemies, and never took sides in a fight. When a dispute arose, he always managed to stay on friendly terms with both parties involved.

There was a man in town who went berserk from time to time. Once he went into the synagogue and took the Torah out of the ark. Then he spit on it and tried to break it apart. This was considered blasphemy, so much so that every Jew in town fasted for days as a result. This man was sometimes violent, and people feared him. The only person in town who wasn't afraid of him was Yossele, and my uncle was the only person this poor man trusted.

During the German occupation of Poland, when it was announced that Jews had to wear bands with a Jewish star on our left arms, we were given thirty days to comply. My uncle did not wait. The next day, he came to our house wearing the band. For a month, he was the only person in town wearing one.

When the Germans ordered all Jews to surrender their furs by a certain date, my uncle went home, picked up all the furs in his house, and delivered them to the designated place right away. Everyone else waited or tried to hide their furs so that the Germans would never find them.

Yossele lived his life with an equanimity and poise that I feel sure he maintained even as he walked into the gas chamber in Auschwitz.

CHAPTER 35: MAKING PEACE
WITH FEAR

"The more I seek security, the less secure I feel."

Fear, with its threatening inner landscape, has been the story of much of my life.

As a boy, I was always afraid of my father's fury regarding my scholastic failures. But the fear I felt as a religious Jew living in an openly anti-Semitic country was more extreme. Would I have been as fearful if I had grown up in a different place and time? I really don't know. When my mother held me in her arms, I'm sure she loved me, but my vulnerable little body must have sensed that her life rhythm was out of step with the cosmic order. I must have absorbed her insecurities and fears.

I only have vague recollections of the early years of my life, but I know I was always scared. When I was very young, I'd seek comfort by climbing into my mother's bed and hiding near her under the blankets. I also followed her around, holding on to her apron for security.

When I was child, I was afraid of many things. I imagined dragons lurking in the dark, and thought they possessed me. Back then I didn't know that it was the other way around.

God scared me, and I constantly worried about the threat of eternal damnation. Since Jewish children were taught that if we saved just one person we would go to heaven, I spent a lot of time daydreaming that I was a strong savior.

I'd learned about the twelve tribes that Moses took out of Egypt. Two tribes made it across the desert, but it was said that when the other tribes tried to cross it, the river threw up stones, preventing them from getting to the other side. This upset me, and I spent a lot of time thinking about what type of contraption I could build to make the river crossable. I wanted to be the hero who saved the tribes and was guaranteed a place in heaven.

Despite the fact that I was scared much of the time, I also appreciated the excitement that came from experiencing fear on my own terms. I risked breaking the rules to go to places that were forbidden, like entering my grandfather's Passover apartment to walk on our roof, or sneaking uninvited into weddings with my friends.

I also couldn't resist attending funerals, even though the cemetery was an hour's walk from town and the burials terrified me. I'd position myself right next to the grave and watch, with great curiosity, how the corpses were lowered into the ground. The bodies were only wrapped in white sheets. There were no caskets. After each funeral, I'd be so afraid I couldn't fall asleep for hours.

When the war was over, I was plagued by terrible nightmares of being back in the slave labor camps. I was drowning in fear, but couldn't understand why. I wasn't able to acknowledge everything I'd lost and all that I'd suffered.

While I tried to present an appearance of calm to the world, inside I endured a state of dread and desperation. During the war, I'd lived with the fear of dying. After the war, I'd lived much longer with the fear of living in a world I saw as cruel and pointless. Fear was always lurking, and I was more afraid of that fear than anything else.

In the early 1970s, when I was just beginning my inner explorations, I had two experiences that taught me something new about the nature of fear. The first happened when I was alone in my jewelry shop. Out of the blue, my hands and feet became red and began to swell up. Soon, I was hardly able to breathe. Every part of me was in immense pain, especially my hands, which were burning unbearably. I had no idea what was going on. Terrified, I began to think it was finally the end of the road for me.

I couldn't stand or walk, but I knew I needed to call for help, so I attempted to crawl to the phone. The pain was so extreme that I collapsed. Lying still on the floor, I just gave up. I stopped resisting the pain and just let it be. I began to breathe into my fear. Even though the sensations I had labeled as pain were still there, the discomfort slowly disappeared. I was able to relax completely, and soon I actually began to feel euphoric. The energy pulsing through me felt like the energy pulsing through the universe. It was glorious.

I don't know how long I lay there, but eventually I was able to get up and walk again. Afterward, I learned that the episode was a severe allergic reaction to penicillin. It was the only time I'd ever taken it. But experiencing the extraordinary shift from pain to pleasure—and from fear to ecstasy—made me realize those feelings weren't complete opposites after all. It was a surprising revelation.

Not long after my penicillin experience, Simon and I went through a scary episode with our business. The Mafia was active with labor unions in the New York area during the 1970s, and one day, out of the blue, a man from the Mafia penetrated our work force and tried to take over our labor union. The man was in cahoots with one of our employees, who managed to talk the majority of his coworkers into signing up. He told them if they joined, Simon and I would have to pay them whatever they asked.

Simon and I decided we were not going to give in to the mob. We knew if we did, we'd be finished. They were killers, and not to be fooled with. So we told the workers that if this proposal went through, we'd close the business—and we meant it.

When he heard the news, the man from the Mafia came to Simon and me and threatened, "Blood is going to run in this building!" Then he directed our workers to go on strike, and they began to picket our shop.

The strike lasted about two weeks. During this time, I went to work every day, and every day I was scared to death, not only for myself but also for my family. I was afraid that the Mafia would do something to the people I loved.

On top of all of these worries, Simon and I felt profoundly betrayed. We'd always cared deeply about the well-being of our employees and paid the highest wages in the industry. I was so upset and angry, I couldn't bring myself to talk to any of the workers. It was difficult for me to even look at them, particularly the guy who'd let the Mafia in.

But sometimes, if you're scared for long enough, something breaks. One day, I felt all my fears disappear. I went into the room where this guy was working, stood calmly in front of him, and looked him in the eye. I looked and looked, and the fear simply wasn't there. I just kept looking at him, and he could tell that something was different. He could sense that I was no longer afraid of him. In fact, I was not afraid of anything.

This wonderful state lasted only as long as I was with this man—perhaps five or ten minutes—but I have never forgotten how it felt to be totally fearless. This employee quit soon after, without giving any reason for leaving. Subsequently, the man from the Mafia who had threatened us disappeared. He just vanished. Nobody ever knew for sure what happened.

—m—

Fear feeds on fear and happiness feeds on happiness. Somewhere along the way, I began to notice a shift: Instead of me trying hard to give up my fear, fear had begun to give up on me. I was no longer easily seduced by fear's fatal attraction.

Yes, there are still nights when the fear creeps back, but when that happens, I don't despair. I know that fear is part of my humanity. When I catch myself worrying, I remind myself that whatever is supposed to happen will happen anyway, and the more I seek security, the less secure I feel.

CHAPTER 36:

FINDING FORGIVENESS

"It's not that I deny the past. I just don't live in it."

One day, when I was in my midforties, I woke up feeling the intense grief and outrage about the Holocaust that I'd been holding back for decades. I jolted straight up in bed, screaming, "NO! This could never have happened. It must be a dream." Neither my mind nor my heart was ready to face the enormity of the humiliation and brutality I'd lived through.

It would be another five years before I'd be able to allow myself to fully feel my grief and mourn for everything I'd lost during the war. When I finally let my tears flow freely, it liberated me from some of the heavy weight I'd been carrying for my whole adult life.

Up until that time, I'd worked through a lot of my feelings, but rarely those directly related to the Holocaust. I'd tried to ignore my terrible nightmares and the awful images I couldn't shake of my parents, brother, and sisters in the gas chamber. Instead of letting myself feel pain and rage about the countless atrocities perpetrated against my people, I was angry at the world, myself, and everyone else. Even now, at this very moment, the Holocaust seems like a horror out of time and place—something my mind cannot, and does not want to, comprehend.

Nonetheless, holding on to my fury for so many decades was draining and painful. It created a darkness within me that was physically and spiritually depleting. I had to find a way to let it go.

I decided it was time to face the people who'd done the killing. I said, "Okay, you won. But just because I'm not the winner doesn't mean I need to be the loser if I don't want to be. I must go on with my life if I want to live at all." I neither forgave nor failed to forgive. I just finally understood that I had to find a way to come to terms with my past. As long as I remained imprisoned by hatred, I'd never be able to fulfill my own destiny.

When I stayed angry with the Germans, whom did it serve? Certainly not me. I was making myself sick while the Germans moved on with their lives. The cycle of hate and revenge has to stop sometime. Why not now? Why not with me?

After the war, it wasn't only the Germans I blamed. I also blamed myself and my people for accepting our fate so meekly, without a struggle. I felt we'd been cowardly, which angered and frustrated me. Looking back, I can see that we were all so terrified, it was as if we were under a hypnotic spell. Nothing we did could have made a difference.

After years of trying and failing to forgive the Germans, I finally realized that my mind couldn't differentiate between anger at others and anger at myself. Until I learned to fully forgive myself, I wouldn't be able to forgive anyone else.

To get better at forgiving, I practiced loving myself every time I made a mistake. Instead of automatically reverting to self-criticism, I'd soothe myself by saying, "It's all okay. I love you no matter what."

How wonderful it felt to bathe myself in tenderness and absolute acceptance! The rotten sweetness of revenge could never console me. Only unconditional love could heal me. My anger was useless in this regard.

—⁓—

Throughout my life, I've repeatedly returned to my memories of that day in the coal mine when I witnessed the large group of Jews walking to Auschwitz. Now, I find it healing to visualize that walk with a different ending—to send out thought forms that foster unity and compassion.

In my mind, I imagine a Jewish girl in the procession who starts experiencing love all around her. At a deep level, she suddenly understands what's really happening: both the Jews and the Germans are living under the spell of their conditioning, and the results are sure to be disastrous for everyone.

The Jews only identify as being Jewish, and the Germans only identify as being German, but it is all an outrageous illusion. This girl knows for certain that all of us are intimately connected. Her clarity gives her so much strength that she finds the courage to stand still and yell, "STOP! STOP! It's not true! Listen to me! Please, listen to me!"

The girl speaks her truth. At first, nobody wants to listen. Everyone thinks she's crazy. But she has such a strong force coming through her that eventually everyone gives her their full attention. She shouts, "They are not Germans. I am not a Jew. This is all a lie. We are all the same. We are all creations of God. We are free to change the course of history!"

One German soldier—the officer of the group—picks up her message. He tells his soldiers, "What this girl is saying is correct. She is telling the truth." The officer's certainty convinces his soldiers, while the girl's clarity and passion convinces the Jews.

The soldiers suddenly look at their captives with fresh eyes, and they no longer see their enemy. Instead, when the soldiers behold the old Jewish men, it's as if they are gazing at their own grandfathers. When they look at the Jewish women, it's as if they are seeing their own mothers and sisters. And when the Jews look at the soldiers, they no longer see monsters—they see their shared humanity.

One by one, the soldiers put down their weapons. They tell the Jews, "Please forgive us. We wish you well. Go in peace."

When I meet a German person now, I try not to let my vision be colored by my baggage from the past. My intention is to meet him in the present moment.

In *this* moment, he is just a person. Instead of automatically associating him with my worst memories, I deliberately make myself look at him with fresh eyes. I remember that despite everything, his essence is pure. Just like me, he was born perfect. Just like me, he learned through imitation, repetition, and force of habit.

It's a conscious act. I do it because it's what I've decided I want to do. I don't do it for him. I do it for me. When I look at the world through the eyes of the past, I am miserable. But when I live in the *now*, unhappiness doesn't exist, because I'm not keeping it alive inside of me.

It's not that I deny the past. I just don't live in it

One day I will die. Before my last breath leaves my body, I expect to ponder the meaning of my life and wonder if it was a journey worth taking. I don't want to carry my bitterness and venom to the grave, or have regrets and sadness fill my heart because of opportunities I lost along the way. I choose to live a life of understanding, compassion, and generosity. I want to take my departure from this world feeling the satisfaction of a job well done.

CHAPTER 37: HAPPINESS

"When I chase happiness, it runs away from me."

When I was sixty-five, my life changed in a wonderful way. I became a grandfather.

Until Myra gave birth to Marea, I could never have imagined how much joy a new baby could bring, especially at my age. Simply holding my infant granddaughter while she slept, watching her stomach rise up and down with every breath, gave me the greatest pleasure.

When my own girls were young, I enjoyed them, but my life at that time often felt overwhelming. Edith was exhausted from raising two small children born only thirteen months apart. I helped as much as I could, often leaving work in the middle of the day when Edith called me at the shop, but my business demanded a lot from me back then. Life often felt like an endless struggle instead of an ongoing celebration.

When Ruthie and Myra were born, I felt as if I'd been entrusted with the greatest of gifts, but I wasn't sure I was worthy. Becoming a grandfather, I got a second chance. It was another opportunity to discover how deeply I could love.

When Marea was only a few months old, Edith and I began to babysit every day for two hours. It became our routine, and we always looked forward to our time with our granddaughter. Soon, being grandparents began to feel like our most important job. I was mostly in charge of the entertainment, and we always had a lot of fun. Every stage in Marea's growth brought its own particular delights.

There was a neighbor next door to Drew and Myra's farm who had a gigantic pig named Penelope. They also had a very friendly horse that Marea and I called Lesley Koo. Walking up the road for a visit with these animals was an important part of our daily ritual. As soon as we approached the fence, the animals would come over to greet us. We always had gifts for them—usually apples or carrots—and if they wanted something more, we would pick the tall grass on our side of the fence and feed it to them.

Marea had three favorite dolls—Little, Middle, and Big. Every day I helped her arrange them in a big circle on the floor, along with her other dolls and stuffed animals, and then carefully cover them all with blankets. For her birthdays, I would make her picture books on my computer, filled with silly rhymes and stories about our animal friends and her trio of dolls.

Being with Marea, I could see very clearly that young children naturally live in the *now.* They are still capable of experiencing life as a spontaneous flow, without the interference of thought. I must have started off that way too, but as I grew to adulthood, I became oriented toward *becoming.* More often than not, I felt pressed for time, as if life was a speeding train whose only purpose was to get *there*—a certain destination that always managed to stay just a little bit ahead of me. The modest pleasures of each day, my enjoyment of the *now*, were traded for an uncertain future. Waiting for tomorrow had become my way of life.

—ɱ—

Happiness wasn't something people ever talked about in Jaworzno, and I never learned how to cultivate it. In fact, almost every time I felt happy as a child, I felt guilty and ashamed immediately afterward. How could I be happy when everyone around me was so somber? I concluded that there was something wrong with me, and in my confusion, I repressed both my joy and my sorrow.

As far as I know, psychology was never discussed in the synagogue, or anywhere else in my hometown. It was only when I came to America that I first heard the idea that people were *supposed* to be happy.

Dear Abby, the syndicated daily advice column in the *New York Post*, ushered me into a new world, one where women and men wrote in to share their problems with the hope of finding a solution. Every day, while I rode the subway back and forth to work, I read about other people's difficulties. For the first time it occurred to me that my emotional pain wasn't so unique after all—perhaps I was just one of many lonely, unhappy people.

I was fascinated to learn that there could be so much suffering in a country as wealthy as America. Clearly, having more wasn't necessarily better. Accumulating material goods wasn't an express lane to happiness.

—◊◊◊—

Growing up, everyone I knew only had dessert on Saturday. It was always very special, and every single bite was savored. One of my biggest surprises coming to America was seeing that most people ate sweets every day and didn't think anything of it.

In Jaworzno, my cousins and I enjoyed the simple games we played in our shared courtyard. I made sabers out of metal from our hardware store, and my cousins and I would play fight. We'd also dig a hole in the ground and roll a ball toward it. Whoever managed to get the ball in the hole the most times was the winner. Sometimes we'd toss beans into the hole instead. We had fun and never expected new or better toys.

But what would have happened if we'd compared ourselves to others and found our toys deficient? Our joy would have been replaced by envy, and the result would have been dissatisfaction.

Whenever I compare myself or my life against my ideas of perfection, I come out the loser. Nothing is perfect—not my family, not my job, not my body. If I have to wait for perfection to be happy, I will surely be waiting forever. The very belief that life *should* be a certain way—that I *should* feel happy—greatly contributes to my unhappiness. When I chase happiness, it runs away from me.

Breaking the habit of living in perpetual dissatisfaction was extremely difficult. At first, I didn't realize that I'd docilely submitted myself to a legacy of pain. I wasn't able to see, much less admit, that a substantial part of me had become addicted to misery. Suffering added drama to my life, filled my conversations, and kept me occupied day and night. My mind even invented problems where none existed.

Seeing the world through the eyes of suffering obscured the glory of my day-to-day life. I couldn't see what a miracle it was simply to be alive. I never stopped to appreciate a bird's song or savor the breeze upon my face. Contentment was nowhere to be found. I had accepted second-class accommodations on this planet without even raising an eyebrow.

To change this unfortunate habit, I began to visualize my self-destructive emotions—fear, anger, guilt, envy, insecurity, and loneliness—as piles of useless baggage. In my imagination, I carefully packed this baggage onto a raft by the shore of a rushing river and secured it tightly with a thick rope. Then I gave the heavy raft a big push and watched it float away. "You've kept me down for years, and I don't need you anymore. Off you go!" I'd holler as I eagerly waved good-bye, feeling light, happy, and carefree.

To teach myself how to embrace joy at every opportunity, I practiced thinking about things that made me feel cheerful every hour on the hour. My goal was to create new grooves in my mind that led to laughter and festivity. It took less than a minute each time, but it helped me shift my awareness to the positive and increased my capacity for delight. My deep intention to let go of my suffering was an essential part of my success in this endeavor.

I believe that we all come to this earth with an endless capacity for joy. Psychological suffering only comes later, because it is learned. And because it's learned, it can be unlearned.

CHAPTER 38: PRESENCE

"I try to do only one thing at a time and never rush."

Back when I was a boy in Jaworzno, time moved more slowly than it does in America today. There was a Yiddish newspaper, but television didn't exist, and my uncle Yossele was the only one in the family who owned a radio. News was mostly shared through letters and men talking in the synagogue. The bench in our family's courtyard was another place where the men congregated to discuss politics.

Jaworzno also got news from a town crier who informed everyone about new laws that had been passed and other significant events. Dressed in a bright red uniform, he would stand in the middle of the market square near our house, bang his drum, and yell, "Hear ye! Hear ye!" to get everyone's attention before making his announcements.

Not that long ago, people weren't assailed by news day and night. They weren't flooded with information about all the bad things that are happening in the world or bombarded with advice about everything they should or shouldn't be doing. Now, even when I turn off the news, I still feel distress in the air.

The healing we get from silence and spending time in nature is becoming increasingly rare, but it's more vital than ever before. Going for a walk on the beach, or looking closely at a tree or a flower, always helps me return to peace. Nature attunes my senses to the divine. Everything I hear, see, and sense is beauty.

—m—

When I was first trying to be more present, the greatest obstacle I faced was the constant chatter of uninvited thoughts in my head. My brain was always active—there was a buzzing noise in the background that never stopped. Whenever I tied my shoelaces, my mind was occupied with something else. While I ate dinner, my mind was in another world. When I walked down the street, my mind was elsewhere. My mind was even distracted while I was making love.

Constant engagement with my thoughts prevented me from experiencing full contact with life. I couldn't enjoy the sweetness, security, and spontaneity that come with being truly united with the world around me. Instead of leading me toward peace, my mind continually led me away from the source of my being, toward loneliness and despair.

It was as if my mind was a defective radio. Every time I turned it on, I heard static and other stations intruding on the same frequency. But since I'd been listening to these unpleasant sounds my whole life, I accepted these constant interruptions as the natural state of affairs. I hadn't yet learned that my conditioned mind continually manufactured distortions that obstructed my ability to experience the beauty all around me. I didn't know that my mind was meant to be a receiving station whose main function was to allow exquisite music to come through loud and clear.

When I couldn't experience the divine firsthand, I doubted its existence and grew increasingly cynical, angry, and depressed. It wasn't until I learned to be present and tune in to the benevolent energies of the universe that I could stop being physically, psychologically, and spiritually undernourished.

Now, my intention is to always stay present. I try to do only one thing at a time and never rush. I live deliberately and appreciate everything—a child's laughter, the texture of a rose petal, clouds floating across the moon in the night sky.

I pay attention from the moment I open my eyes in the morning and gaze out my window at the beautiful mountains. I stay present as I get up, put on my clothes, and walk downstairs to the kitchen to make hot cereal for breakfast. I put water in the pot, add oatmeal when it begins to boil, and stir it every so often as it cooks. When my breakfast is ready, I sit in a chair and eat slowly, right from the pot—and in that moment, I don't do anything but eat. I look at my food and enjoy the smell, texture, and taste of it.

Myra recently gave birth to my grandson, Jeffrey, and I treasure every moment with him. I stay present as we crawl through his plastic toy tunnel, dig holes in the sand, and even when he cries inconsolably.

Presence is where peace lives. It doesn't matter what I'm doing. Nothing is too small or unimportant. Making oatmeal is my meditation. Folding laundry is my meditation. Mending holes in my socks is my meditation.

Of course, there are still times when I feel sad and wonder why, but then I consciously return to the present moment. As soon as I stop worrying about the future or ruminating about the past, I can reconnect to the wisdom that resides within me. Once again, I am able to access a deep trust and find happiness in the little, everyday moments of my life.

When I am fully present, there's a shift in my frequency that enables me to access a new way of seeing the world. My old energy is washed away and replaced by a new energy, which is always love. It is a state of grace in which barriers of thought melt away and peace becomes endless. I know that I existed before time was born and that I am eternal. I welcome each day as a glorious adventure, and know simply being alive is magical.

CHAPTER 39: COMING HOME
TO LOVE

"We are all connected by love, and our heart as our center of gravity is always our truest and most helpful guide."

We all take journeys and make discoveries. Like all true journeys, mine was internal and external, chronological and timeless, physical, mental and spiritual. It covered much territory, but it was not direct.

I am grateful that even through such dense, stifling darkness, I was able to perceive the bare whisper of my inner voice telling me, "Life is worth fighting for, no matter the price." Otherwise, I would have perished.

That whisper brought me hope that there could be more to my life than struggle and frustration. It inspired my determination to go all the way, to never buckle under the avalanche of self-doubt, fear, and pressure to conform. It gave me the courage to release the old and useless so I was free to build a new life—one based on trust, beauty, and peace.

Nothing hurts as much as having an identity formed by a fear-based belief system. Using willpower alone, I was unable to change these patterns. Battling my thoughts made me their prisoner, and resisting my emotions energized them. Until I realized that my mind didn't have all the answers, I was attacking the problem, not the root cause. By itself, my mind could never create the wholeness necessary for healing.

As I look back over my life, I feel certain that my human experience on earth—starting with a seemingly endless sea of pain, fear, rage, guilt, grief and loneliness—could not be the consequence of my present lifetime alone, the Holocaust notwithstanding.

My efforts to make my own existence saner have led me to believe that as a whole, human beings have not yet reached our emotional or spiritual maturity. Perhaps our task here on earth includes not only an attempt to resolve the difficulties of our own lives but also an effort, no matter how small, to change humankind's pattern of development so that we can all become more harmonious and loving.

I often wonder if the mechanical mind is just a passing state in our evolution, a midway station between matter and spirit. Could it be that the suffering we endure on this planet is the very thing that forces us to raise ourselves to a higher state so that we can overcome the limitations of time and space and become one with the original creative force? Is it the hungers within us that create our need to return home to the source of our being?

The most important thing I have ever done is to become an explorer of my mind and heart. I got to know myself as I really am, rather than who I imagined myself to be. No one else could have deciphered the subtleties of my own mind. No one else could have faced my repressed emotions, heartbreaks, and fears.

Through self-observation, the more mature, dispassionate part of me examined my conditioned self without condemnation, apology, or guilt. I created an atmosphere of self-love and forgiveness that allowed the fearful child in me to be comforted and grow strong. Over time, I began experiencing the boundless peace and joy that resides in the depth of my being—feelings no one can ever take away from me, because they are not dependent on conditions outside myself. Finally, I was able to taste true freedom. My heart rejoiced. I had come home to love.

My journey may seem unique, but I believe I represent humankind as a whole. Within myself I have discovered all the ills that beset the human race—pettiness, cruelty, selfishness, and foolishness. I have also found the sorrows that we all share, as well as kindness, love, and understanding.

I believe we are all children of a benevolent cosmos, and at the core of our being, each one of us is the divine individualized. Everything is made of energy; nothing is isolated. We are all connected by love, and our heart as our center of gravity is always our truest and most helpful guide.

Happiness is our birthright, freely given to us all as an act of grace. We don't have to do anything to deserve it. Like the sun, mountains, and warm summer rains, happiness belongs to everyone.

Beyond the confines of our limiting belief systems, a magical world is waiting for all of us.

MYRA'S EPILOGUE: NOW THAT
YOU KNOW MY FATHER

From where I stand now, it's hard to believe that I didn't fully appreciate my father's writings while he was alive. I try not to feel too badly about this. I was very preoccupied with my own busy life, and in truth, I simply wasn't ready to learn from him yet.

My father had faith that everything happens for a reason, so I'm choosing to trust that this is the best time for his story to make its way out into the world. Maybe it's more important to share it now, when there are so few Holocaust survivors left to tell their stories. And perhaps my father's messages of compassion and peace are particularly relevant at this moment in time when so many of us are trying to steer the world in a more unified and loving direction.

During his lifetime, Mendek lived his revelations quietly, pouring all that he was eager to share directly onto the page. I'm so grateful he took the time to do so, and that I was lucky enough to become his posthumous partner in creating this book.

Not even my mother knew that her husband had such a robust inner life. When I gave her an early draft of this book to review for accuracy, she couldn't put it down. To avoid all interruptions, she turned off her phone and refused visitors. The first thing she said to me when she finished reading was, "You made me fall in love with your father all over again."

While he was still alive, my sister, Ruthie, was the only person in our family who truly understood that our father experienced life from a higher plane. She lived with my parents for two years while struggling with a debilitating illness, and this gave her a unique opportunity to see our father embody his philosophy, moment by moment. Despite Ruthie's worrisome situation, which put her and our mom in a state of panic and grief, our father was always able to maintain his inner peace and optimism. He brought smiles and light into those dark years.

Ruthie's favorite part of sharing a home with our father was watching him dance. Our dad was especially enchanted by music, and whenever he heard a beautiful song, he'd stop whatever he was doing and really listen. Then he'd dance, his movements becoming ever more enthusiastic as he swayed in ecstasy, free of all inhibitions.

When Ruthie knew he'd be passing by her door, she often played music to lure him in. Within moments, he'd begin to dance. She told me, "I loved to watch him go into an altered state and get blissfully carried away by a song. He'd feel the energy of the music and his breathing would change. His body would start moving in his own unique way. He often jumped in a circle, reminding me of Sufi mystics. He'd laugh, stomp his feet, and shake his head while reaching for the heavens. I've never seen anything like it."

Over the course of his life, my father concluded that conforming to society's expectations about how a grown man should behave would never lead him to happiness. He stayed true to himself and did what he liked, which only served to make him more beloved. It took me a long time to realize what a miracle it was for a man with his history to be so happy and free.

In addition to his intelligence, patience, and persistence, part of what made Mendek such a successful inventor was that he never assumed that just because something had always been done a certain way, that it was the right way or the best way. He loved to create new things and took great satisfaction in making anything better than it was before. Whether it was devising a bracelet clasp or figuring out how to handle his repetitive thoughts, my dad held a perpetual certainty there was a better method waiting to be discovered.

The limitations most of us take for granted—the ones we don't even realize exist—were the very obstacles that fueled my father's imagination. Just like the universal key he invented as a little boy, he was energized by the challenge of breaking through all barriers. My father would not be confined.

—⟋⟋⟋—

No one in our family can pinpoint when Mendek first showed signs of his illness, but one day, when he was in his late seventies, he found himself driving the wrong way on Carmel Valley Road. We all agreed that it was time for him to stop driving, so my parents moved to a condominium where they could walk or take the bus everywhere. Friends who saw my parents around town would always tell me how sweet they were together: a gray-haired couple holding tightly to each other's hands, talking nonstop, as if they were newlyweds.

My dad still seemed healthy when my sister got married in February 2001. Ruthie's daughter Nina was born in June of 2002, and my parents were thrilled to have another baby to care for almost every day. But it was around this time that my dad began coming home from the store without the items he'd been asked to buy, and soon he was getting lost on his way to routine destinations.

When my father's symptoms worsened, my mom took him to their family physician, who told her that Mendek had Alzheimer's disease. My mother refused to listen to all the terrible things she should expect. Instead, she decided to enjoy every moment with her husband without the worries that come with projecting a terrifying future.

—⟶ɯ—

For a few years after his diagnosis, my father's passion to write accelerated. He began to spend most of his day in the office he'd fashioned for himself in his garage, writing continuously. He also carried a pen and paper in his pocket at all times and continued to jot down revelations as they came to him.

Eventually, my dad needed around-the-clock supervision. He could pick any lock and would leave the house and wander. Fortunately, we were able to place him in a care facility only one block from my parents' apartment. The first time we toured it, he asked the staff, "Is the food here kosher?"—even though he hadn't kept kosher for seventy years.

My mother brought my father home from the care facility for a visit every day, and sometimes I was the one to get him and walk him over. The women who worked there often told me how much they loved my father, and that he was their only patient who didn't complain. Some even brought their children in to play with him.

I liked to help my dad get ready because he made everything silly and fun. We'd put on his shoes, and also his coat; he didn't like being cold and wanted to wear a warm coat even in the summer. We'd hold his jeans up with red suspenders, and he'd wear either his blue or tan sun hat, depending on his mood.

On these walks, I often tried to get my father to move faster, but he always refused to be rushed. We'd sing his favorite songs as we strolled at the very slow pace he stubbornly set. He would stop repeatedly to look closely at the flowers along the way, and he'd stop to gaze at the verdant hills in the distance, asking me who lived there.

Once we arrived at their house, my dad's favorite thing to do was sweep the leaves off the patio. When he was done sweeping, he'd sit in his chair and enjoy gazing at the trees and plants.

My father would often hold a flower in each hand and look at them from different viewpoints—holding them low and then high. He'd smell them repeatedly, then smile and shake his head in wonder. Once in a while, he tried to explain how wonderful it felt to be surrounded by so much beauty. My mother would help him find the words.

As his Alzheimer's progressed, my father slowly went back in time. His memories of the present day and the recent past faded until he no longer remembered moving to California. Soon, he also forgot his life in New York.

What my dad did remember was his hometown of Jaworzno and his family there. In fact, the reason he recognized me for so long was because I looked like them. I was the only one to whom he would say, "I remember you from my kitchen table in Jaworzno." Other days he would look at me adoringly, shake his head, and say, "I love you so much, but I don't know why." I found that a beautiful way to be loved.

Although my mother remained his anchor until the very end, there were days when he didn't recognize her. The first time he asked her who she was, she said, "Who do you think I am?"

"The housekeeper?" my father guessed.

"No," she replied, "I'm your wife."

Mendek looked at the gray-haired, eighty-something-year-old woman standing in his doorway with much surprise. Then he gave her a glorious smile and exclaimed, "I am so lucky!"

My father's final writings were simple, and memory was one of his most frequent themes. "Remember to be loving, forget to be unloving," he wrote, and "Forget to be fearful, but remember to be cheerful." Even when his memory was almost entirely gone, my dad still read his positive affirmations over and over. He carried them on little pieces of paper in his pockets and placed them all over his room at the care facility so they were always within reach.

With no possibility of artifice, the way my dad lived his life confirmed that the transformation he'd begun decades before was complete. When Mendek had completely forgotten most of his life and rarely even remembered his own name, he kept focusing his attention on all that is joyous and beautiful.

My father's last words were "cheerful" and "Edith."

A SELECTION OF
MENDEK'S WRITINGS

Mendek's Prayer

May the storms of my everyday existence—my sadness, loneliness, and fear—become the springboard to awaken me to a wisdom greater than my own, so that I may learn the lessons of love, joy, and freedom forever and ever. Amen.

Mendek's Poems

Yesterday

For the greater part of my life, I labored in pain.
I wanted to be happy today, yet I hung on to yesterday.
Yesterday, in my memory, I am a lost little boy, the image
of parent and child, my initiation into helplessness.
Yesterday is the image of an imperfect world, holding
on to my fears, the suffering of the human race, the
Holocaust revisited.
I want to be happy now.
Why then do I hold on to yesterday?
Take away my yesterday, and I am like the day I was born.
I am as God created me.
My mind is silent.
I am at peace.

Paradox

When I want nothing, I have everything.
When I need nothing, I feel rich within.
When I don't try to be happy, I'm happy anyway.

Flying

While my body is restricted by the limits of the physical
universe,
While my conditioned mind is restricted by the limits of
time, space, and habits,
It is my privilege to reach for the clouds and, riding high,
It is up to me to overcome the limitations of matter and soar
into freedom.
It is my privilege to fly.

I Was Born Free

I was born free.

I can live in the past and suffer the consequences, or choose to live in the now and be happy.

I was born free.

I can be angry and complain, or rise above all limitations.

I was born free.

I can dwell on imperfections, or choose to see the good in myself and others.

I was born free.

I can live a life of pretense, or I can dare to be myself.

Wind Guide

What if I let myself be spontaneous, as if the wind was my guide?
What if I let the blossoming flowers show me what to do?
What if I asked a growing tree to show me the way?
I can't regulate existence or push the river, but I can rest my mind in the light, and let the truth guide me.

Blessings in Disguise

God gives me what I need.

Anger, depression, and fear remind me that my life needs mending, that there is something about myself I don't want to know, feel, or face.

I can learn to embrace all of my feelings.

I can accept and love my inner child, with all his pain, grief, and trembling insecurity.

I trust that God gives me what I need.

Now, because of my fear and darkness, I am able to see the light.

Freedom

My ideas and values have a life of their own.

Their existence has their roots in my conditioning and culture.

I cannot claim that they originated within me.

Yet I think I am free.

My emotions have a life of their own.

They swell up and recede, like tides of the sea, with a rhythm not of my own making.

Yet I think I am free.

My actions and reactions have a life of their own.

I'm often unaware of the "whys" of my own behavior, doing things unlike "me."

Yet I call myself free.

My thoughts have a life of their own.

They follow each other, like night follows day, without acknowledging my authority.

Yet I call myself free.

Your World, My World

Your inner world perceives and creates an outer reality
that is uniquely your own.
My inner world perceives and creates an outer reality that
is uniquely my own.
Each of us sees the sky differently.
Who then wants the responsibility of passing judgments
on someone else's world?
Who believes they can play God?

On Life and Love

The young want to experience it
The rich want to buy it
The thief wants to steal it
The scholar wants to debate it
The dictator wants to control it
The scientist wants to explain it
The fearful want to escape it
The fool wants to manipulate it
The wise just allow it to be

The Happiness Road

Walk freely and joyfully on the happiness road, where
trees grow tall and flowers blossom.
Find the sanctuary deep in your heart where happiness
abides.
You are as important to the sun as the sun is to you.
Know yourself as love.

Affirmations

A Beginning

I choose to believe that wonderful things will come about,
somehow, some way.
And when they do, I will be astonished and pleased.
As a matter of fact, I am pleased already.

I Love Myself

I love myself, and then I love myself again, and again, and again.

When I love myself in the morning, and even more at night, I begin to love myself all day long.

And then I find that I can love others too, and soon there is no room for fear.

I Go For It

I want all that is delightful and makes my heart rejoice.
I choose that which is beautiful and makes me smile.
I embrace all that is loving and kind.
I go for what inspires me to sing, dance, and celebrate life!

Now is a Good Time

Now is a good time to be happy. There is never a good time to be unhappy.

Now is a good time to be cheerful. There is never a good time to be fearful.

Now is a good time to be loving. There is never a good time to be unloving.

My Own Nurse

I am my own nurse.
I heal my wounds with tenderness and care.
I comfort myself with love and understanding.
I cure my sorrows and loneliness with compassion and forgiveness.
I heal my wounds and restore my health so that I can be free and fearless.
I live fully, smile fully, and love fully once again.

My Inner Riches

There is music within me. I dance to it.
There is laughter within me. I delight in it.
There is wisdom within me. I honor it.
There is grace within me. I flow with it.
There is joy within me. I smile with it.

A New Day

I breathe in forgiveness, I breathe out blame.
I breathe in humility, I breathe out arrogance.
I breathe in joy, I breathe out sorrow.
I breathe in light, I breathe out darkness.

Patience

I can wait . . .
Because in waiting, I learn patience.
I can wait . . .
Because in waiting, I learn strength.
I can wait . . .
Because in waiting, I learn faith.

Mendek's Visualization Exercises

Color Visualization

Using color was one of my favorite visualizations. Here's an example of the type of exercise I devised and practiced every day with a different color:

I relax deeply.

Rest

I visualize the color blue.

Rest

In my mind's eye, I see the color blue filling the room and embracing all space.

Rest

I experience the color blue becoming bluer, warmer, more pleasing and more cheerful.

Rest

I experience the color blue becoming even bluer, even warmer, even more pleasing and more cheerful than ever.

Rest

I allow the color blue to embrace me with its warmth, love, and goodness.

Rest

I allow the color blue to caress me with its warmth, love, and goodness.

Rest

I allow the color blue to wipe all my cares away.

Rest

Waterfall Visualization

I imagine standing under a waterfall and letting the running water caress my body, from the top of my head to down past my toes. I feel my worries wash away, and gladly let them go. I do as many or as few of the following visualizations as I feel like in one sitting, and I'm always adding new ones.

The waterfall is washing my anger away.
The waterfall is washing my insecurities away.
The waterfall is washing my illusions away.
The waterfall is washing my pride away.
The waterfall is washing my loneliness away.
The waterfall is washing my worries away
The waterfall is washing my guilt away.

Basket of Flowers

I am a carrier of love offerings. I carry a basket of flowers, and I offer one to everyone I meet, be they friend or foe. No matter how many flowers I give away, more flowers appear in the basket. It is magic. I am a part of this magic.

Growing Tree

*I see a tree growing taller, getting stronger, and blossoming.
It spreads its branches reaching out to the world, high up to
the sky.
I am the tree.
The tree is me.*

Mendek's Ego Scan

When my ego wins, I lose, because my ego cares more about what others think than it does about how I feel. It cares more about how well I'm performing than how much I'm enjoying the experience. My ego is always trying to make me be the person it thinks I should be.

One day, I sat down and made a list of the behaviors I exhibit when my ego is in charge:

- Having pride in my ideas and accomplishments
- Being a slave to routine and convention
- Comparing myself to others
- Worrying about my image and reputation
- Repressing and denying my feelings
- Feeling sorry for myself
- Indulging in impatience, irritation, and intolerance
- Desiring things I don't really need, such as compliments and being right

Then I made a second list—the ways I behave when I am living from my heart:

- Cultivating humility, patience, and forbearance
- Knowing that life isn't about winning
- Not being intimidated by my fears
- Daring to be different
- Practicing self-honesty, prayer, and meditation
- Being flexible and willing to change my ideas
- Giving up my ego's ideas about what happiness and love are all about

For more of Mendek's writings, inspiration, resources for healing, and much more, please visit **QuestForEternalSunshine.com**, and follow us on Facebook and Instagram @QuestForEternalSunshine.

ACKNOWLEDGMENTS

I could fill a whole book expressing my gratitude to the dozens of people who helped make this unique project possible. Although my thanks to each of you must be brief, please know that my appreciation for your time, interest, and essential contributions is immense.

I owe my deepest gratitude to my father, Mendek Rubin. Dad, I am so grateful you had the urge to write—to chronicle your amazing life and spiritual journey. I could never have predicted that we would write this book together or that it would be one of the most transformative experiences of my life. I am in awe of you and feel immensely proud and blessed to be your daughter.

I thank my mother, Edith Rubin, for contributing her stories and memories, which are a huge part of this book. Mom, I am grateful for all the ways you supported this project, and for the love and care you showered on Dad throughout his life. He adored you and knew how lucky he was to have found you. Your love story is the most beautiful one I know.

I am immensely grateful to my sister, Ruthie Rubin-Harmer, for your memories and insights, your video and audio recordings, and all the essential content you contributed. I couldn't have created this book without you. Thanks to you and your remarkable daughter, Nina Harmer, for taking on our social media initiatives and for generously employing your many talents to share Mendek's wisdom with the world. Thanks also to my brother-in-law, Stephen Harmer, for your video interviews of Mendek decades ago and shared recollections.

Bronia Brandman, thank you for being an insightful, open-minded, honest, and supportive aunt, collaborator, and Holocaust educator. I am grateful for your memories, stories, knowledge, and perspective, as well as the countless hours you put into this project doing lengthy interviews, reviewing copy, answering questions, and connecting me with other family members. One of the greatest blessings of this book is that it has made us close friends forever.

Thanks to my cousin Etta Brandman for being an early reader and always making me feel like an appreciated family member. And to Etta's husband, Harry Klaristenfeld, thanks for your kind, generous words of appreciation, and for helping me improve the accuracy of facts relating to Judaism and Jewish culture.

An effusive posthumous thank-you to Simon Geldwerth—my father's cousin and business partner—who was always "Uncle Simon" to me. In addition to rescuing my father and aunt from desolate conditions in post-war Germany, supporting them in every way for years, and then making my dad's business success possible, Simon diligently tracked down every possible keepsake originating from Jaworzno for my dad and Bronia, and also preserved every significant letter and document throughout his entire life. All of these gems provided vital content for this book. Because he had the foresight to collect and safeguard photos of our family when he fled Europe, I am able to know what my grandparents, aunts, and uncles looked like, and also what my father and Bronia looked like as children. My gratitude to Simon is boundless.

To Simon's daughters—my cousins Mizi Zoltan and Mati Sprecher—thank you for your warmth and generosity. Your memories, along with the abundance of family treasures you shared, provided significant content for this book, and I appreciate all your valuable edits and honest feedback. Mizi, thanks for going above and beyond in so many ways: patiently educating me about our family's history, reading and rereading all the copy I sent your way, translating documents, and catching my many mistakes.

—m—

It gives me great pleasure that this book gave me the opportunity to get to know many cousins who also trace their roots back to Jaworzno. I appreciate your many kindnesses, memories, and photos, as well as the time you spent reviewing this book.

Judy Hager, I will never forget my exhilaration at hearing about your trips to Jaworzno where you'd dug in the Jewish cemetery in search of our mutual great-grandfather Elias's tombstone the first time we spoke. Thank you for your friendship and devotion to researching our mutual past, as well as the precious photos and stories you shared.

I am deeply grateful to Mila Kornwasser for contributing many essential facts about our family's hometown and relatives there. And also to cousins Joe Kornwasser and Betty Ryzman for the lovely chats and recollections you shared.

Thank you to Beth Bass for your kindnesses and for connecting me to your brother, Robert Willner. Robert, thank you for all the time you spent reading copy and fact finding, and especially for your help with our family tree. I could never have created it without you. It has been an honor to work with you in an effort to preserve our shared history, and I will always be grateful for your keen and generous contributions.

Myra Farrell—you were one of my most exciting discoveries: a second cousin who shares both my name and many of my interests. Thanks for your friendship, help with this book, and for connecting me with our mutual cousin, Mimi Berkowitz. Mimi, thanks so much for sharing the priceless autobiography of your grandmother, Sarah Gutfreund, who spent her girlhood summers at Elias's farm in Jaworzno.

To my cousin, Sheryl Rosenberg, thank you for your sweet reminiscences about our fathers' love for each other, your great photos, and the open-hearted way you welcomed me into the family. And thanks to Oliver Rosenberg for your stories about the time you and your grandpa visited Jaworzno, your fascination with our family's history, and the wonderful discussions we had in Monterey.

To my cousin Izzy Mintz, thank you for being so warm-hearted, for sharing family stories, and for telling me the book "knocked your socks off." Thanks, too, to Izzy's sisters, Selena Mintz and Betty Wicentowsky, for the great conversations and precious photos.

—∭—

I've been very fortunate to have a magnificent group of gifted women help me birth this book. I will be forever grateful for your assistance and guidance:

Patrice Vecchione—talented writer, poet, artist, and teacher—thank you for your great edits and ideas, and for holding my hand throughout the first year, when I was confused and floundering. You fanned the flames of my passion, and your sage advice helped guide me.

Cecelia Cancellaro—wise, experienced editor and dear family friend who knew my father and appreciated his kind heart and unique approach to life—thank you for being my editor and advisor throughout this entire journey. I greatly value all the help and support you've provided, and your boundless patience with my unending revisions.

Laura Davis—the teacher from my fateful first writing work-shop at Esalen two months after my dad died—you opened my floodgates, and then became my mentor, collaborator, and frequent rescuer. Thank you for turning me into a writer, helping me navigate so much new terrain, and generously sharing your brilliance, creativity, and unrelenting drive. You are the only person who has ever pushed me harder than I push myself. This book would not be here without you.

Toni Burbank—the legendary editor who got my manuscript midway through the project, and immediately knew how to whip it into shape—I feel lucky to have had the chance to work with you. Many thanks for making the book so much better, and many thanks also to the wonderful Jack Kornfield for connecting us.

Hilary Nicholls—remarkable healer and spiritual mentor—you are an angel on earth and my dad would have adored you. I will be forever grateful for your devotion to this project. You not only helped it achieve its potential, you also kept my confidence and enthusiasm fueled throughout.

Brooke Warner—cofounder and publisher of She Writes Press—I feel very grateful for the opportunity to publish this book with you. You are a dedicated pioneer with a powerful vision who is helping many women writers reach an audience and achieve their dreams. Thanks to the entire She Writes Press team, especially my project managers, Cait Levin and Shannon Green, and creative director Julie Metz. And thanks also to my "She Writes sisters" for your constant encouragement and the expertise you so generously share. I feel very lucky to be part of such a special and supportive community of women writers.

I am deeply thankful to the many people whose talents contributed to this book in diverse and crucial ways:

Bryn Anderson, for catalyzing this whole project by expertly typing out my dad's original manuscript—diverse fonts, unconventional layout, and all.

Alan Stacy, for designing the working manuscript and managing the content for inserts. You've been a pleasure to work with, and I greatly appreciate your patience, insights and frequent timely rescues.

Maya Pollack, for the family trees, custom map, and for

managing the video shoot with Bronia. I feel lucky to have had someone so enthusiastic and competent as my research assistant. I hope you know how much I adore and admire you!

Ronni Sweet, for interviewing my parents so long ago, and then locating the recording for me. Without you, I never would have known that you could find coal under the earth anywhere you dug in Jaworzno, and many other special details.

Annie Kagan, for your bull's eye instincts, applying your genius to this book, and for your uncompromising commitment to excellence. I am exceedingly grateful for your generosity.

Jill Mangino for your wise guidance and important insights.

Crystal Patriarche, Keely Platte, Madison Ostrander, and Hanna Pollack—my team at SparkPoint Studio—for being such wonderful publicists.

Tina Powers—extraordinary "reporter from the other side"—for the priceless conversations with my father, your love and enthusiastic support, and for helping to open my eyes to other worlds.

Bonnie Wirth—wise, wonderful woman with a clear, powerful connection to spirit—for setting me straight on important issues in my life and for the messages from my father, especially about the book's title.

Katie Dutcher—webmaster & digital marketing manager—for sharing your skills and wisdom. It's always a pleasure to work with you.

Rachel Schiff for your great ideas and appreciation of this project.

Liz Dubleman—book launch marketing consultant—for sharing your impressive expertise.

Oren Rudavsky—exceptional filmmaker and director—for the priceless footage of Bronia Brandman and Judith Saly for the book's website.

Clare Redden and Zelda Greenstein—two very talented film editors—for helping tell my family's story in such a compelling way.

Deenie Rose, from Rose Studios, for the wonderful Hilary Nicholls recordings and your beautiful flute music.

Alli Elliot, from Alli Pura Photography, for your great work and the pleasure of your company.

Barrett Briske and Krissa Lagos, for expert editing and excellent ideas.

Jolanta Kulinska—Polish researcher and translator—for working hard to gather information on my family from Jaworzno and discovering "The Kingdom of Elias."

Nick Block—for translating my family's letters and artifacts from the original German and Yiddish into English.

Sue Peccianti, owner of my local UPS store, and her wonderful employees, Sara Peccianti and Iris Smith, for your help printing and shipping dozens of books for me over these many years.

Kathy Whilden and all the folks at Brown Bag Zen in Monterey, who have supported me as I've been finding my voice with this project, and who've appreciated my dad and his journey.

Thomas Hübl and Tirzah Firestone, for the important healing work you are sharing with the world, and for your deep wisdom on intergenerational trauma that is very powerful and illuminating.

Josefa Rangel and Cain Carroll, for all the ways you have supported my health and healing, which has also enabled me to better understand my father's journey from darkness to light. Working with you has been one of the greatest privileges of my life, and my gratitude is boundless.

—ɯ—

This project brought me back in touch with some old friends from the Pathwork who have been incredibly open-hearted and supportive of this project:

Charles Rotmil, thank you for generously sharing the amazing photographs of my dad. You captured his essence, as well as the feel of Pathwork in the 1970s. It is only because of you that we have photos of my dad and Simon at "the shop." I am also immensely grateful for the wealth of memories you shared.

Thank you to the entire Saly family for your continued friendship, kindness, and steadfast support. Judith, thank you for the love and warmth you've shown me, for reviewing the book, and sharing so many stories. I am thrilled we were able to capture your beauty and wisdom on film. Alan Saly, thank you for sharing memories, reviewing multiple drafts of this book, clarifying Pathwork philosophy, coordinating the video shoot, and for your appreciation of my father's wisdom and story. Camilla Saly, heartfelt thanks for memories, insightful edits, and all the delicious food. And thanks to Silver Saly for your recollections and kindness.

Reina Gilson—the talented artist who illustrated my dad's "Higher Self Cards"—thank you for sharing your cards, memories, wisdom, and appreciation for my dad and this book. And a huge thanks to your husband, George Gilson, for his interest in this project, catching typos everyone else missed, and most generous feedback.

Sonia Gluckman, for your great interest in this project and Holocaust trauma resolution, as well as your support, memories, and fast friendship.

I feel immense gratitude toward everyone who has read the manuscript over the years: Trudy Anderson, Joanne Ashe, Paul Cahalan, Prana Carpenter, Christine Coke, Daya Fisch, Ellen Fondiler, Avi Geldwerth, Lipa Geldwerth, Jill Goodman, Julie Goodman, Kathy Goodman, Trudy Goodman, Lynn Hirshfield, Oona Hull, Kyra Hurwitz, Bedri Jahmurataj, Laurie Kleinman, Sarah LaCasse, Eileen LaMothe, Janet Lesniak, Mara Lopez, Jane Marcus, Charles and Karen Osborne, Marian Penn, Suzanne Rafer, Andrea Ruizquez, Debra Silverman, Will Smith, Susan Turner, and Janna Jo Williams.

—᷈᷈—

An extra-special thanks to those of you who were immensely generous with your time, edits, and feedback. Some of you wrote out pages of suggestions, or read parts (or all) of the book repeatedly as I continued making revisions. I am deeply touched and appreciative. Your assistance helped me in countless ways, and you are owed many thanks:

Samantha Cabaluna and Naomi Pollack—for your insights and encouragement regarding multiple versions, which grounded the book in the real world; Cynthia Cahalan and Laurie Benjamin—especially for your clear compass on the introduction and final essay; Darren Starwynn and Mitchell Winthrop—for your generous feedback, important edits, and invigorating encouragement; Lisa Rudolph and Atara Berliner—for asking great questions that broadened my perspective and led me to add important new content; Chloe Friedland and Martin Reiser—for your zeal, insights, dog love, and delicious food; Robert Greenfield, for your appreciation of this story and the numerous other ways you supported me; Mark Bauman and George and Sherrill Ash—for forming an insightful, valuable focus group at a critical stage; Nancy and Gordon Wheeler—for your appreciation and thought-provoking feedback; Rita Rosenkranz—for the time you spent on this project, and especially for adjusting my course to one my dad would have chosen; Patricia Wolff—for deeply appreciating the value of my father's journey and wisdom, and for turning an early draft into your book club selection (what a special evening); Darryle Pollack—for brilliant insights and notes I cherish—you are always in my heart; Maureen Manning—for multiple reads and fabulous ideas that greatly impacted the project (we might not have ended up with the maps and Bronia videos if not for you); Jenny and Joseph Jedeikin—for your support, which buoyed me, and for valuable input at two critical stages; Jack Sherman—for your intelligent observations, clear vision, and great edits; Elliot

Ruchowitz-Roberts and Debbie Sharp—for sticking with me for years, reading version after version, and sharing sage advice, and for Debbie's precious memories from working with my dad and interviewing my parents; Terra Tirapelli—for being an amazing healer who supported me, physically and emotionally, through all my challenging trips to New York City while working on this book; Ann Packer—for essential feedback, encouragement, and enthusiasm during the homestretch, just when I needed it; Rabbi Leah Novick—for sharing your memories and wisdom, and being a spiritual pioneer; Nikiko Masumoto, for your heartfelt support, being a huge inspiration, and for sharing the journey of being apprenticed to our fathers; and Mort Levitt—for helping my dad with his writing decades ago, saving his work all these years, and then tracking me down to give it to me. I am immensely grateful for all the treasures you preserved.

—ɷ—

Finally, I want to thank my immediate family:

Henry and Oscar, my Labrador family members, for your wonderful company and dogged determination to making sure I took regular farm walk breaks to stretch my back and clear my head while writing this book.

Drew Goodman, beloved husband, for your many insightful contributions and the countless ways you have generously supported me and this project. I am deeply grateful for you and the beautiful life we've built together.

My children, Marea and Jeff Goodman, for all the memories you contributed, and for being brilliant, insightful editors. I am immensely gratified to have preserved your grandfather's story and revelations for you and your future offspring in this book. I hope it helps you feel your grandpa's love and wisdom, which always surrounds you.

ABOUT THE AUTHORS

MENDEK RUBIN was a Holocaust survivor and brilliant inventor who helped revolutionize the jewelry manufacturing industry, generating numerous patents in the 1960s and 1970s. After he retired from the jewelry business, he invented the initial equipment used to wash and package baby greens for Earthbound Farm—the first company to successfully market ready-to-eat salads for retail sale. Mendek also applied his genius to his own psyche, creating innovative ways to overcome the trauma of the Holocaust and live a truly joyous life. He is the author of two books: *Why Not Now*, a book of poems and prose, and *I Am Small, I Am Big: The Way We Choose to Live*, a book about positive thinking written for children. A self-taught artist and nature photographer, Mendek died in September 2012 in Carmel Valley, California, at the age of eighty-seven.

MYRA GOODMAN is a well-known pioneer in the world of organic food and farming and the author of three cookbooks. In 1984, she and her husband, Drew, founded Earthbound Farm, which became the largest grower of organic produce in the world. The Goodmans have been credited with helping to bring organic food to the mainstream, and Myra was one of four farmers chosen by the James Beard Foundation and US Department of State to represent the United States in a prominent "conversations" video at the entrance to the US pavilion at the 2015 World's Fair. She has appeared on national television shows, including *Oprah*, *Regis & Kelly*, and *Good Morning America Health*, and has been featured in hundreds of publications, including *People* magazine, the *Costco Connection*, *More*, *Forbes*, *The New York Times*, and *AARP*. Myra and Drew have two grown children and continue to live on their original farm in Carmel Valley with their three yellow labs, Oscar, Henry, and Leo.

Mendek Rubin author photo © Rubin family archives

Myra Goodman author photo © Alli Pura Photography

SELECTED TITLES FROM SHE WRITES PRESS

She Writes Press is an independent publishing company founded to serve women writers everywhere. Visit us at www.shewritespress.com.

Jumping Over Shadows: A Memoir by Annette Gendler. $16.95, 978-1-63152-170-6. Like her great-aunt Resi, Annette Gendler, a German, fell in love with a Jewish man—but unlike her aunt, whose marriage was destroyed by "the Nazi times," Gendler found a way to make her impossible love survive.

Braided: A Journey of a Thousand Challahs by Beth Ricanati, MD. $16.95, 978-1-63152-441-7. What if you could bake bread once a week, every week? What if the smell of fresh bread could turn your house into a home? And what if the act of making the bread—mixing and kneading, watching and waiting—could heal your heartache and your emptiness, your sense of being overwhelmed? It can.

Note to Self: A Seven-Step Path to Gratitude and Growth by Laurie Buchanan. $16.95, 978-1-63152-113-3. Transforming intention into action, Note to Self equips you to shed your baggage, bridging the gap between where you are and where you want to be—body, mind, and spirit—and empowering you to step into joy-filled living now!

Think Better. Live Better. 5 Steps to Create the Life You Deserve by Francine Huss. $16.95, 978-1-938314-66-7. With the help of this guide, readers will learn to cultivate more creative thoughts, realign their mindset, and gain a new perspective on life.

Surviving the Survivors: A Memoir by Ruth Klein. $16.95, 978-1-63152-471-4. With both humor and deep feeling, Klein shares the story of her parents—who survived the Holocaust but could not overcome the tragedy they had experienced—and their children, who became indirect victims of the atrocities endured by the generation before them.

At the Narrow Waist of the World: A Memoir by Marlena Maduro Baraf. $16.95, 978-1631525889. In this lush and vivid coming-of-age memoir about a mother's mental illness and the healing power of a loving Jewish and Hispanic extended family, young Marlena must pull away from her mother, leave her Panama home, and navigate the transition to an American world.